Praise for

stickyfaith

This is one of the most important books on this subject *ever*.
Kara Powell and Chap Clark are some of the finest youth
experts in the world. I admire and respect their work and
their passion to make a difference. Don't miss reading this
significant book. It is very hopeful, yet challenging.

—JIM BURNS, PhD, president of HomeWord;
author, *The Purity Code*, *Confident Parenting*,
and *Teenology*

Having served in churches with teenagers and college-age
young adults for more than twenty years, I can tell you that
Sticky Faith addresses the questions and concerns we all have
about how to help children and youth develop a long-lasting
vibrant faith after high school. I cannot recommend a book
on this topic more highly than this one, and I wish it had
come out twenty years ago!

—DAN KIMBALL, author, *They Like Jesus
but Not the Church*

Anyone interested in the future of the Christian movement
in America will want to be informed by the insights of *Sticky
Faith*. Hopefully this book will help move us toward what
should be happening at church, at home, on campus, and on
mission trips to build faith into the next generation.

—REGGIE MCNEAL

Hand-me-down Christianity may last for a season, but in the long run, it fails to stick. What we as leaders and parents are in desperate need of is a navigation system that will direct us in how to cultivate a generation of young people who authentically own their faith. Kara Powell and Chap Clark have provided us with such a resource. As a parent and church leader, trust me, this is a book you'll return to over and over again.

—BRYAN LORITTS, pastor,
Fellowship Memphis

The single most important variable in the spiritual nurture of kids is, without a doubt, parents. To be honest, we parents have been doing a rather dismal job of carrying out this God-given role. Kara and Chap not only issue a much-needed wake-up call but also offer practical suggestions for nurturing a real and vital lifelong faith that is integrated into all of life. Parents, what you don't know *can* hurt your kids. *Sticky Faith* will help you love and nurture your kids into a faith that lasts.

—WALT MUELLER, president,
Center for Parent/Youth Understanding

stickyfaith

Everyday ideas to
build lasting faith
in your kids

Dr. Kara E. Powell
& Dr. Chap Clark

ZONDERVAN

ZONDERVAN.com/
AUTHORTRACKER
follow your favorite authors

We want to hear from you. Please send your comments about this book to us in care of zreview@zondervan.com. Thank you.

ZONDERVAN

Sticky Faith
Copyright © 2011 by Kara E. Powell and Chap Clark

This title is also available as a Zondervan ebook. Visit www.zondervan.com/ebooks.

This title is also available in a Zondervan audio edition. Visit www.zondervan.fm.

Requests for information should be addressed to:

Zondervan, *Grand Rapids, Michigan 49530*

Library of Congress Cataloging-in-Publication Data

Powell, Kara Eckmann, 1970 –
    Sticky faith / Kara E. Powell and Chap Clark.
        p.   cm.
    Includes bibliographical references.
    ISBN 978-0-310-32932-9 (softcover)
        1. Christian teenagers — Religious life. 2. Parenting — Religious aspects —
    Christianity. 3. Child rearing — Religious aspects — Christianity. 4. Christian education
    — Home training. 5. Parent and teenager — Religious aspects — Christianity. I. Clark,
    Chap, 1954 – II. Title.
    BV4531.3.P67   2011
    248.8'45 — dc22   2011008920

Cover design: *Extra Credit Projects*
Interior design: *Beth Shagene*

Printed in the United States of America

---

12 13 14 15 16 /DCI/ 23 22 21 20 19 18 17 16 15 14 13 12 11 10 9 8 7

To my mom,
who modeled Sticky Faith for me every morning,
coffee cup in one hand and Bible in the other
—Kara

To Chap, Rob, and Katie,
your spiritual journeys have taught us
what Sticky Faith looks like in action
—Chap

contents

foreword

Tom is a high school freshman at our church who is similar to others his age. He loves sports and girls, and his life is trapped in a perpetual cycle of homework and busyness. By all accounts, he is a normal high school kid.

But Tom has something that makes him different. He is being pursued by a church that is dedicated to prepping its entire congregation to encourage faith in young people. We fail a lot at Menlo Park Presbyterian Church, but one of our key goals is to have many adults who know and love kids like Tom and point them to Jesus Christ. It isn't just a ministry strategy; it's the theological conviction that this is what the church is called to be.

Recently, Tom ran into a thirty-year-old member of our church named Mike, and they laughed and talked for a few minutes. When the conversation ended, Tom turned to his mom and said, "Mom, I will always follow Jesus."

Nothing could have meant more to this mom. "Why?" she said.

"Because there are so many guys like Mike at our church who I know love me," he said. "I want to be like that."

Kids experience Jesus Christ when adults in the church

give them grace, time, and genuine love with no hidden agenda.

But here is the sad reality: Tom is the exception, not the norm. Most kids lack connection to and investment from a church community that is mobilized to reach them. Very few churches have transformed their culture to see kids as a mission field on their own campuses.

No one has diagnosed and communicated the heart of this problem like Chap Clark and Kara Powell.

To say that Menlo Park Presbyterian Church's philosophy has been influenced by the work and thought of Chap Clark and Kara Powell is a massive understatement. Chap and Kara are leading the way forward in thoughtful, theological reflection about kids and faith in today's changing landscape. These are some of the deepest thoughts you will read about today's kids and their faith.

But what is so helpful about this book is its immensely practical help. Kara and Chap are in constant dialogue with "real world" youth workers. Turning theory into concrete practice matters to us. It matters to Tom too, although he may not realize it yet. And it matters to anyone who dedicates their time, energy, and even their whole lives to seeing young people embrace Jesus Christ at the core of who they are.

Chap and Kara have a dream that kids like Tom eventually will be the norm, not the exception. *Sticky Faith* is more than another book about kids and their faith; it's a journey into the heart of every adult who is forced to respond to the question of what, really, the church of Jesus Christ is called to be.

—JOHN ORTBERG AND JIM CANDY

acknowledgments

The insights found in these pages result from the collective work of a phenomenal team of parents, grandparents, researchers, youth leaders, and Fuller students. Special thanks to Dr. Cameron Lee for his steady consultation and leadership throughout this process, to Brad Griffin and Dr. Cheryl Crawford for their invaluable insights and contributions to the research, to Dr. Chloe Teller for keeping the team on track, to Dr. Erika Knuth for crunching so many numbers, to Irene Cho for keeping the Fuller Youth Institute (FYI) running while we were preoccupied with this project, and especially to Dr. Krista Kubiak Crotty for asking the initial question that launched this whole adventure.

We'd also like to thank others who have served as part of the FYI staff and research team during this process, including Cody Charland, Nikki Chase, Emily Chen, Rana Choi Park, Marianne Croonquist, Kris Fernout, Dr. David Fraze, Mike Hensley, Andrea King, Melanie Lammers, Dr. Lydia Mariam, Meredith Miller, Paul Walker, and Matt Westbrook.

This book was made much better because of the input of wise friends and parents who took the time to give us feedback, including Dave Powell and Dee Clark (we wanted to mention them first), as well as Roger and Lilli Bosch, Cindy Go, Toben Heim, Kathy Hernandez, Jeff and Jenny Mattesich, Christa Peitzman, and Adam and Nancy Stiles.

FYI wouldn't exist without other enthusiastic Advisory Council members and passionate supporters, including (but not limited to) Dale and Mary Andringa, Noel Becchetti, Barbara Bere, Jim and Judy Bergman, Max and Esther De Pree, April Diaz, David and Carol Eaton, Sted and Robin Garber, Walter and Darlene Hansen, Megan Hutchinson, Ken Knipp, John Lewis, Mark Maines, John and Chris Mumford, Brian and Linda Prinn, Sam and Betsy Reeves, Roy and Ruth Rogers, Albert Tate, Jeremy Taylor, Ron and Sharon VanderPol, Gabe Veas, Mike and Valerie Volkema, Scott Watt, Dale Wong, Jeff Wright, the Tyndale House Foundation, the Servants Trust, the Thrive Foundation, the Vermeer Charitable Foundation, and the Stewardship Foundation. A special, heartfelt thanks to both the Lilly Endowment for funding much of our Sticky Faith research as well as Wally Hawley for his invaluable coaching and many pearls of wisdom.

Your work has stuck with us and we are eager to see how the Lord builds even more Sticky Faith in kids.

the not-so-sticky-faith reality

*My parents are probably
the biggest influence out of anybody.*
—Robyn

*Both my mom and my dad have spent hours and hours
and hours through my life talking to me about what
it means to be a Christian, what it means to follow God,
and what that should entail and how to do it.*
—Billy

Tiffany had failed to turn out like Phil and Amy had hoped.

Like most parents, Phil and Amy had great visions of who their daughter would become as she entered high school and college.

Their expectations were high in part because Tiffany's first steps down the yellow brick road of adolescence showed great promise. As a ninth grader, Tiffany was deeply committed to knowing Jesus and making Jesus known. While friends shared horror stories about their kids' sullen attitudes, moodiness, and flagrant disregard for family rules,

Tiffany was generally pleasant and obedient. Tiffany had lots of friends, but she also enjoyed being with her parents. And Phil and Amy enjoyed being with her.

From the first Sunday that she walked into the high school ministry at the church where I (Kara) served as one of the youth pastors, Tiffany plunged into every church activity possible. Any event that was offered—youth choir, beach days, weekend service trips to Tijuana—Tiffany was there. Not only was she there, but she usually showed up to church at least thirty minutes early to see if she could help.

And help she did. Tiffany was especially good at making posters. She would spread paper across the youth room floor and try to come up with creative images to promote upcoming events or reinforce the teaching topic for the next week. When we made posters together, we talked about our mutual desire to know Jesus and help others know him too.

Sure, Tiffany wasn't perfect, but the other youth group parents envied how easy Phil and Amy seemed to have it with their daughter.

Around eleventh grade Tiffany started to change. She began to wear dark, heavy makeup.

Her skirts grew shorter. A lot shorter.

Phil and Amy found themselves locking horns with Tiffany over her wardrobe.

Soon they found themselves locking horns with Tiffany over just about everything. Grades, curfew, friends—everything was a battle.

Tiffany no longer came early to church. When I asked her if she wanted to help with posters, she said she was too busy. Throughout Tiffany's senior year, her involvement at church grew more and more sporadic.

Six months after Tiffany graduated from high school, she became pregnant. Confused and ashamed, she wanted nothing to do with our church. Or me.

Phil called me from the hospital the day Tiffany gave birth to her son. Although Tiffany had avoided me during her pregnancy, I asked her dad if she would be okay with my visiting her that day and meeting her son. She said yes.

Phil, Tiffany, and the new baby were together in the hospital room. After we chatted for a few minutes, Tiffany offered to let me hold her son. It was the first time I had ever held a baby who was only a few hours old. I told her so, and she grinned.

Phil tried to grin, but I could see the deep sadness in his eyes. He looked at me and I knew what he was thinking, because I was thinking it too.

Why did Tiffany's faith—a faith that seemed so vibrant at first—fail to stick?

Kids' Faith Isn't Sticking

Parents and churches are waking up to the harsh reality that there are more Tiffanys than we had previously realized. The board of the National Association of Evangelicals, an umbrella group representing sixty denominations and dozens of ministries, has passed a resolution deploring "the epidemic of young people leaving the evangelical church."[1]

But is it really an epidemic? Does the data suggest that kids' exit from the faith is more like a trickle, or a flood?

As we have examined other research, our conclusion is that 40 to 50 percent of kids who graduate from a church or youth group will fail to stick with their faith in college.[2]

Let's translate that statistic to the kids you know. Imagine your child and his or her friends standing in a line and facing you. (I'm sure they are smiling adoringly at you.) Just like you used to do on the playground to divide into teams, number off these kids, "one, two, one, two, one, two ..." The ones will stick with their faith; the twos will shelve it.

And they'll be making the decision about whether to shelve their faith after your most intensive season of parenting is over.

I'm not satisfied with a 50 percent rate of Sticky Faith.[3]

Are you?

I doubt it.

Here's another alarming statistic: only 20 percent of college students who leave the faith planned to do so during high school. The remaining 80 percent intended to stick with their faith but didn't.[4]

As has been rightly pointed out, young adulthood is often a season of inevitable experimentation for teenagers who were raised in the church and are learning to make the faith their own. That hunch is supported by the encouraging statistic that somewhere between 30 and 60 percent of youth group graduates who abandon their faith and the church return to both in their late twenties.[5] Yet those young adults have already faced significant forks in the road regarding friendship, marriage, vocation, worldview, and lifestyle, all while their faith has been pushed to the back seat. They will have to live with the consequences of those decisions for the rest of their lives. Plus, while we can celebrate those who eventually place their faith back in the driver's seat, we still grieve over the 40 to 70 percent who won't.

College Students Gone Wild

From the movie *Animal House* to the Asher Roth song "I Love College," college life has been depicted as a nonstop merry-go-round of sex, drugs, and alcohol, with a few hours of study thrown in here and there. Granted, sex, drugs, and alcohol are not the ultimate litmus test of a college student's spirituality. (We'll say more about that later.) And of course, media portrayals of college kids are certainly exaggerated. Nonetheless, since more students are partying than we might realize and since students' partying often affects their relationship with God, it's a factor of Sticky Faith we have to discuss.

Each month, just less than 50 percent of full-time college students binge drink, abuse prescription drugs, and/or abuse illegal drugs.[6] According to one analysis conducted by a professor of public health at Harvard University, the number of fraternity and sorority members who binge drink has climbed to 80 percent.[7]

This heavy alcohol consumption is costing students—a lot. According to one estimate, college students spend $5.5 billion each year on alcohol—more than they spend on soft drinks, tea, milk, juice, coffee, and schoolbooks combined.[8]

This widespread use of alcohol opens the door to the bedroom. Dr. Michael Kimmel, professor of sociology at State University of New York, has researched college behaviors extensively and has concluded that "virtually all hooking up is lubricated with copious amounts of alcohol."[9]

You've almost certainly heard the term *hooking up*, a phrase that refers to a multitude of sexual behaviors ranging from kissing to oral sex to intercourse, without any expectation of emotional commitment. College seniors have an average of nearly seven hookups during their collegiate careers, with 28 percent of them hooking up ten times or more.[10]

Kimmel vividly captures the wild tone of college campuses by explaining the effects on local health care: "Every single emergency room in every single hospital adjoining or near a college campus stocks extra supplies on Thursday nights—rape kits for the sexual assault victims, IV fluids for those who are dehydrated from alcohol-induced vomiting, and blood for drunk driving accidents."[11]

Christian Kids Gone Wild?

What about kids who come from Christian families? Are they as wild as the rest of college students?

The good news is that multiple studies indicate that students who are more religious and/or more likely to attend church or religious gatherings are less likely to consume alcohol or hook up.[12] Yet just because religious kids are less likely to party doesn't mean that they aren't partying at all. In a pilot study we conducted early in our research, 100 percent of the sixty-nine youth group graduates we surveyed drank alcohol during their first few years of college.

One member of our Sticky Faith research team, Dr. Cheryl Crawford, focused her research on kids who had been designated as leaders in their youth ministries in high school. After extensive conversations with these former student leaders, Dr. Crawford concluded that "loneliness and the search for friends seem to push the buttons for everything else. The primary reason students gave for participating in the 'party scene' was because that's where 'everyone' was. One student told me, 'I don't think I've met many people who don't drink here. It's really hard to meet people if you don't drink.' These key decisions about partying are made during the first two weeks of students' freshman year."

Partying and other challenges in transitioning from high school to college were described well by one college senior we interviewed: "Transitioning out of high school into college is like you're leaving on a giant cruise ship. You're heading out of this harbor and everyone's waving you off. Let's say this ship is your faith. As soon as you start sailing out to this new port called college, you realize you're in a dinghy. You don't have this huge ship, and you're completely not prepared, and your boat is sinking! Unless there's someone with a life raft who's ready to say, 'We got you. Come right here. This is where you can be, and this is where you can grow,' you're done."

Steps to Sticky Faith: Our Research

At the Fuller Youth Institute, we want to partner with you to offer your kids a stronger ship of faith and extend a life raft to those who feel like they are already drowning. In all of our research initiatives, our mission is to leverage research into resources that elevate leaders, kids, and families.

I've been parenting for ten years and serving kids in youth ministry for twenty-five. My coauthor, Chap Clark, has been parenting for thirty years and serving in various forms of youth, family, and pastoral ministry for, hmm, a few more years than I have! While that adds up to a lot of years of experience, we wanted to pair our experiences with insights from several additional research paths.

The first research path began with Chap's spending

most of a school year on a public school campus as a substitute teacher with permission to be a participant-observer researcher on campus. In his work, Chap recorded stories and other observations and sorted them first into impressions and then into coded conclusions. At the same time, a research team worked to integrate and compare Chap's findings with what other experts had written on adolescence.

Following this, Chap conducted twelve focus groups across the US and Canada, and in the end published his study in the book *Hurt: Inside the World of Today's Teenagers.*[13] Chap and his team of Fuller Seminary faculty and students continue to study and interview kids, and many of the insights in this book come from that research.

The second research path was my work on the College Transition Project, a series of comprehensive studies of more than five hundred graduating seniors.[14] You'll hear from these students (with fictitious names) through quotes in sidebars and at the start of each chapter. The six years of research by the College Transition faculty and student team have been fueled by two research goals: to better understand the dynamics of youth group graduates' transition to college, and to pinpoint the steps that leaders, churches, parents, and seniors themselves can take to help students stay on the Sticky Faith path.[15]

> For more on the questions we asked
> in our surveys, please see the appendixes
> as well as *www.stickyfaith.org.*

In many ways, the students in this long-term study represent typical Christian seniors transitioning to college (e.g., they come from different regions across the United States, they attend public, private, and Christian colleges and vocational schools, and 59 percent are female and 41 percent are male). Yet the kids in our sample tend to have higher high-school grade-point averages and are more likely to come from intact families than the typical student heading to college. We also recruited kids from churches that have full-time professional youth pastors, which means they are likely to come from bigger-than-average churches (average church size was five hundred to nine hundred people). From the outset, we want to admit that these factors bring a certain bias to our findings, which we diligently tried to counter by examining other research studies and by conducting face-to-face interviews with students with more diverse academic, family, and church backgrounds.

In an effort to bring focus to our College Transition Project, we recruited high school seniors who intended to enter college after graduation, whether a four-year university, a junior college, or a vocational school. We can't be certain, but we think it's likely that our findings are relevant to those graduates entering the workforce or the military. Our hunch has been supported by one parallel study indicating that church dropout rates for college students and noncollege students are not significantly different.[16]

Sometimes we get asked about gender differences when it comes to Sticky Faith. While we have not extensively explored this question, we can say that in our study, overall there were no strong differences between men's and women's faith based on the measures we used.

Defining Sticky Faith

As we were initially conceptualizing this research, we quickly ran into one important question: what exactly is Sticky Faith? While it's tempting to apply former Supreme Court Justice Potter Stuart's famous definition of obscenity as "I know it when I see it," that doesn't fly in academic circles. Based on the research literature and our understanding of students, we arrived at three descriptors of Sticky Faith; the first two are relevant for all ages, while the last has heightened importance during students' transition to college.

1. *Sticky Faith is both internal and external.* Sticky Faith is part of a student's inner thoughts and emotions and is also externalized in choices and actions that reflect that faith commitment. These behaviors include regular attendance in a church or campus group, prayer and Bible reading, service to others, and lower participation in risky behaviors, especially engaging in sex and drinking alcohol. In other words, Sticky Faith involves whole-person integration, at least to some degree.

2. *Sticky Faith is both personal and communal.* Sticky Faith celebrates God's specific care for each person while always locating faith in the global and local community of the church.[17] God has designed us to grow in our individual relationships with him as well as through our relationships with others.

3. *Sticky Faith is both mature and maturing.* Sticky Faith shows marks of spiritual maturity but is also in the process of growth. We don't assume that a high school senior or college freshman (or a parent, for that matter) will have a completely mature faith. We are all in process.[18]

The vast majority of kids we interviewed—even those who thrived in college—reported that college was both a growth experience and challenging, full of new perspectives and experiences. Reading through the transcripts, it seems that the typical college student sits down at a table full of new and interesting worldviews and people. Instead of allowing faith to be merely one of many voices clamoring

> In college I think my faith finally got really serious to me. God is so real, and so important in my life. My faith finally got hard and inconvenient, which I think makes my faith real.
>
> —Shelby

to be heard, those with Sticky Faith had determined that their faith would sit at the head of the table.

Parents' Central Role in Sticky Faith

Much of this chapter has been bad news. Chap calls me an eternal optimist. I don't mind that label. So let me give you some good news from our research: your kids are more connected to you than you might think. We asked graduating seniors to rank five groups in terms of the quality and quantity of support they received from them. Those five groups were friends inside of youth group, friends outside of youth group, youth leaders, parents, and adults in the congregation.

Which group did they rank number one? Parents.

More good news: our research shows a relationship between this parental support and Sticky Faith.

But parental support, while important, is not the only way you influence your child. More than even your support, it's who you are that shapes your kid. In fact, it's challenging to point to a Sticky Faith factor that is more significant than you. How you express and live out your faith may have a greater impact on your son or daughter than anything else.

After his nationwide telephone survey of 3,290 teens and their parents, as well as after conducting 250 in-depth interviews, Dr. Christian Smith, a sociologist from the University of Notre Dame, concluded, "Most teenagers and their parents may not realize it, but a lot of research in the sociology of religion suggests that the most important social influence in shaping young people's religious lives is the religious life modeled and taught to them by their parents."[19]

> My parents are my spiritual role models in every way; it is my goal to develop myself spiritually as they have.
>
> —Tyler

As Christian Smith more simply summarized on a panel with Chap and myself, "When it comes to kids' faith, parents get what they are."[20]

> To access the audio of this panel with both of us and Christian Smith, visit www.stickyfaith.org.

Of course, there are exceptions. Your faith might be vastly different from your parents' faith. Plus, I've met plenty of parents whose kids end up all over the faith spectrum.

Nonetheless, a major reason Chap and I wanted to write this book was our deep desire for kids to journey through life with the God who loves them more than they can even imagine. You are more than a launching pad for that journey; you are also an ongoing companion, guide, and fellow journeyer.

"Sticky Findings" and "Sticky Faith Made Practical"

We have divided each chapter into two sections, the first of which is called "Sticky Findings." In that first section, we summarize what we've learned from the kids we have studied, as well as from our ongoing exploration of Scripture. As researchers who are Christ-followers, we are convinced that simply crunching numbers about students' experiences will leave us splashing around in the shallow end. It's when we pair our study of students with a thorough examination of theology and Scripture that we are able to dive into deeper waters.

For the last few years, we have been discussing these Sticky Findings with parents through one-on-one consultations, focus groups, and nationwide seminars. We invited twenty-eight innovative churches from around the US to apply our research to their settings by joining our Sticky Faith cohorts. Through two summits and monthly webinars, these churches became diverse incubators for Sticky Faith ministry. From what we have learned from parents at these churches, as well as from a host of other churches of various sizes, denominations, and geographical locations, we can recommend a robust list of practical parenting ideas. Those ideas are described in detail in the second section of each chapter, labeled "Sticky Faith Made Practical."

> I can't emphasize enough how much of an influence my parents had on me, and the more people I am around, the more people I get to meet whose parents didn't influence them in the same way my parents did.
> —Chet

It's Never Too Late

If you're a parent or grandparent of teenagers or college students, you might be asking yourself if it's too late to develop Sticky Faith in your kids. Hear this good news: because faith development is a lifelong process for all of us, it is never too late to be more intentional in your parenting and the faith you model and discuss with your kids.

Having said that, we suggest that if you are starting late in the process, go slowly. If you sound a Sticky Faith siren and immediately launch into a long list of new Sticky Faith parenting practices, your kids' antennae will sense this as fake and forced. Instead, be more cautious and organic. Choose a few new rituals to try, and if they don't go all that well, abandon them and try something else. Your older kids will be much more receptive if you slowly start to turn up the volume on the way you discuss and model Sticky Faith.

It's Never Too Early

Early in our research, we concluded that building Sticky Faith doesn't start when your kids are seniors, or even juniors. The reality is that your kids' faith trajectories are formed long before twelfth grade. While we have devoted chapter 7, "A Sticky Bridge out of Home," to discussing how to build Sticky Faith in your high school seniors, we encourage you to apply the rest of the book to your younger kids too. My three children are five, nine, and eleven years old, and our research impacts the way my husband and I parent every day. Chap's kids are twenty-three, twenty-six, and almost thirty years old, but he and his wife, a marriage and family therapist, have been applying these principles along the way as they have discovered them.

In fact, you'll be more likely to develop Sticky Faith in your kids when you share our research with other friends, parents, grandparents, and especially with your church. Try to create as broad of a Sticky Faith team as possible. After studying seniors' transition to college, Dr. Tim Clydesdale, associate professor of sociology at the College of New Jersey, concluded, "Given the seeming importance of retaining youth for most religious groups in the United States, it is striking how haphazardly most congregations go about it."[21] That's why we spend quite a bit of time not only giving you parenting tips but also providing tips for churches on how to disciple their young people into a solid, maturing faith. And because the church is *you*, we hope you will introduce these findings to your congregation and look for ways to implement them in your relationships, worship, and activities.

It is time to end the haphazard way we prepare our kids for all they will face in the future.

Above the Research: A Loving and Faithful God

As much as we wish there were a foolproof plan for Sticky Faith parenting, we will be the first to admit that there isn't. During this research, we've met parents with amazing faith and parenting skills whose kids had shelved their faith, and we've met spiritually lukewarm parents whose kids were on fire. There is no Sticky Faith silver bullet. There is no simple list of steps you can take to give your kids a faith that lasts. Part of what makes parenting so demanding is that easy answers are rare.

That might be disappointing, but let us make a few additional admissions that we hope will encourage you.

> As much as we love research, we will also be the first to admit that we love God more.

> As much as we believe in research, we will also quickly admit that we believe in God more.

> As much as we value sorting through data, we value prayer far, far more.

As we share our research with parents, including parents who are grieving the way their children have strayed from the Sticky Faith path, we are repeatedly reminded of the God who transcends all research and all easy answers. We are struck by how much we need to depend on God for wisdom and strength for ourselves, and sometimes just plain miracles for our families. Ultimately, the Holy Spirit, not us, develops Sticky Faith in kids.

In one of our Sticky Faith parent presentations, one heartbroken mom told the group that she had been on her knees praying that God would draw her kids back to his love.

Upon hearing this, a mom sitting nearby said that she was doing more than praying on her knees. She had spent so much time praying for her kids, lying prostrate before the Lord, crying out for him to intervene, that the floor had left a mark on her forehead.

Another mom once told me that she never realized how much control she would lose over her kids when they became teenagers. She told me, "The more control I lost, the more I craved to pray."

Through our research, our nationwide conversations with kids and parents, and even our own parenting, we have learned much about Sticky Faith. We are full of suggestions. But our top suggestion is this: trust the Lord with your kids and continue to ask — maybe at times beg — the Lord to build in them a Sticky Faith.

sticky reflection and discussion questions

1. When people decide to read a book, usually they are trying to solve a problem. What problems are you hoping to address by reading this book?

2. How would *you* define *Sticky Faith*?

3. How does it make you feel to think that you are the most important influence on your child's faith?

4. As you think about how you've parented thus far, what have you done that has contributed to your kids' faith? What do you wish you had done differently?

5. What do you think of the suggestion that parents trust the Lord with their kids and beg the Lord to build Sticky Faith in them? Perhaps you'd like to put this book down and pray for a few moments before you even turn the page.

the sticky gospel

God is not the friend he was in high school.
He is now more like the grandparent in the home
that I visit only on holidays or special occasions.
—Ely

My parents were both raised in Christian families,
but how they shaped me had a lot more
to do with being a cultural Christian than being
in a personal relationship with Jesus.
—Geoff

Darrin was a good kid, from a good home, who had grown up going to church. When he started coming to our youth ministry, he was more interested in who was there than in growing in God. The summer he went to camp, however, everything changed. Darrin soon got serious about his faith (as he described it) and became an overnight leader who not only encouraged others in their faith but was diligent in living out everything a youth leader or parent would want in a young disciple. He read his Bible every morning, even memorizing Scripture. He kept a prayer journal. He gave talks at church and volunteered for any and every need. Darrin was, in short, as committed a Christian kid as any.

Then he went to college.

The first week of school, Darrin found a group of friends and instantly bonded. He said he thought about going to church, but after a few weeks of enjoying some of the newly discovered opportunities of college life, he lost interest. I (Chap) called him and tried to meet with him the first weekend he came home, but he was too busy to connect with me or even to come to church. By the next summer, Darrin told me he wasn't sure if "this God stuff" was even real, or if it "worked," and regardless he wanted to wait until after college to "get back into it."

That phrase "get back into it" should have set off a warning bell in my mind, because it illustrated what faith had been to Darrin. During high school, his faith was real, of that I have little doubt. But it turned out to be a shallow, performance-based faith that was focused on Darrin's being "into it" or Darrin's "working" to have it make sense. In a matter of months, Darrin had moved from being a committed Christian leader to being someone who had left the faith behind. He hadn't realized that the ultimate point of the spiritual duties he practiced was something much deeper.

Kara and I think that the core of Sticky Faith is developing a clear and honest understanding of both the gospel and biblical faith. As our kids are led into an awareness of their significant role in the kingdom of God demonstrated throughout Scripture, they will have the best chance of discovering a faith that is compelling and life-giving.

Sticky Findings

Many Kids Are Unable to Define Christianity

Many of our kids—even those who have grown up in church —have surprising views of what it means to be a Christian. We asked college juniors who were youth group graduates this question: "What would you say being a Christian is all about?" More than two-thirds listed answers related to "doing" the faith, like "loving others" and "following Jesus' example." More than one-third did not even mention Jesus, and of those, 35 percent did not mention God *or* Jesus! Certainly being a Christian involves an outcome of love and service, but is this work the central definition of faith?

While in high school, Darrin perceived that his job as a believer was to live up to the challenges and expectations of his parents, church, and Christian friends. He equated faith with spiritual disciplines, "good works," and living as an example of Christianity that would please God. But in Darrin's case, and for many other kids as well, that lifestyle of external faith is not enough to sustain Sticky Faith.

Many Kids Have Adopted the "Gospel of Sin Management"

When your children are taught what it means to live as a Christian, typically they receive a list of what to do and what not to do.

Do go to church and youth group as often as possible, read your Bible, pray, give money, share your faith, get good grades, respect your elders, spend spring break on a mission trip, and be a good kid.

Do not watch the wrong movies, drink, do drugs, have

sex, talk back, swear, hang out with the "wrong crowd," go to Cancun for spring break, or go to parties.

Philosopher Dallas Willard coined a phrase that sums up the way too many of us think of faith, calling it the "gospel of sin management": "History has brought us to the point where the Christian message is thought to be essentially concerned with only how to deal with sin: with wrongdoing or wrong-being and its effects. Life, our actual existence, is not included in what is now presented as the heart of the Christian message, or it is included only marginally.... The current gospel then becomes a 'gospel of sin management.'"[1]

Kids are not picking up this gospel of sin management in a vacuum. They are learning this gospel from us—from the gospel we believe, talk about, and, most important, model to them every day. Our kids are mirrors of our attitudes and beliefs.

Kids Need to Discover What It Means to Trust Christ

At the heart of Sticky Faith is a faith that trusts in God and that understands that obedience is a *response* to that trust, in everything. The Greek word for *faith* is *pisteuo* (pronounced "Pis-tay-U-o"). In the New Testament, *pisteuo* can be translated as three different but closely related words: "faith," "believe," and "trust." So as a general rule, when we see the words *faith* or *believe* in the Bible, they come from *pisteuo* and thus can also be translated as "trust." As you help your kids understand Sticky Faith, every decision, every thought, and every action comes down to this: in whom do I place my trust? Do I trust my instincts, my desires, my convictions, or do I trust in Christ?

Jesus affirmed this when he was asked, "What must we do to do the works God requires?" Jesus answered, "The work of God is this: to believe [or trust, *pisteuo*] in the one he has sent" (John 6:28–29). In Christ, that is the primary and central calling God has for our kids—and for us—as we develop our faith.

In contrast with assuming it's our "doing Christianity" that makes faith work, the Sticky Faith process described by Paul shows that the way we deepen our trust is to put ourselves in a position to draw close to God even while the Holy Spirit is pursuing and surrounding us. Paul's point in Galatians 5:6 that "in Christ Jesus neither circumcision nor uncircumcision has any value" is not limited to circumcision or any of the other ancient Hebrew rituals. It also applies to our contemporary attempts to climb the ladder of righteousness on our own through our self-imposed gospel of sin management. We can insert any of today's devotional duties that we say are the essence of faith into Paul's phrasing in Galatians 5:6. "For in Christ Jesus," for example, "neither reading the Bible nor not reading the Bible has any value" *in and of itself!*

Spiritual disciplines do not make us righteous because we do them, but rather they put us in a position to be drawn into trusting Christ more fully. If we or our kids are reading Scripture (or doing any devotional duty) because we think we will somehow in the course of our studying become more righteous, we are in effect saying that we don't need God to change us. In contrast, the Sticky Gospel reminds us that our focus is to trust, and God promises to work within us at every stage of the process—by strengthening our trust, by giving us peace and patience as we wait for our lives to be transformed, and by actually changing us from the inside out.

The theme of focusing first on internal transformation instead of external behavior is echoed by Paul in Philippians 3:1 – 14. Paul calls his circumcision and his zealous pursuit of righteousness based on the law "garbage" compared with knowing Christ. In Philippians 3:12, Paul writes that he will "press on to take hold of that for which Christ Jesus took hold of me."

The outcome of a faith that is more concerned with working than trusting, or doing rather than freely living, is dangerous to young disciples. As we saw with Darrin at the start of the chapter, a performance-based Christianity can last only so long. When kids reach the awareness — through failure or pain, or insecurity or inner wrestling with who is the owner of their faith — that they do not have the power or interest to keep the faith treadmill going, they will put their faith aside.

To help our kids discover and grab hold of a sustainable, long-term, and vibrant Sticky Faith, we must stay true to the words of Jesus and heed the council of Paul: trust in the one the Father has sent, and live convinced that the only thing that counts is faith expressing itself through love.

Paul describes our role in this Sticky Gospel in Galatians 5:5: "For through the Spirit we eagerly await by faith the righteousness for which we hope." Or to put it in a simple equation, faith/trust plus waiting on God to change us equals righteousness.

We may not say this outright, but it is so easy to slip into the kind of faith that says, "God loves you, sure ... but he'll *really* love you when you [fill in the blank]." Galatians 5:5 reminds us that it is God's job to work in us and to present us as righteous, and it is our job to learn to trust him and let the process of becoming the quality of person he created, redeemed, and called unfold.

As parents, then, instead of concentrating on — and sometimes fretting about — whether and how our kids are living "righteous" lives, we have the opportunity to help them discover, access, and strengthen their trust and faith in Jesus Christ. In so doing, the righteousness they eventually display will be the product of the Holy Spirit.

> I realized that I was believing something that I had been taught. I had to learn to own my faith and to understand why I believed what I believed. I had to learn to say what that was about — who God is, what he's done in my life, why I put my faith in him.
>
> —Lanz

For some of us, trusting this process in our kids can be hard. We tend to want outcomes that are immediate and measurable. When our kids don't seem to get what we think they ought to know or do or be, we can easily fall into a "because I told you to, that's why!" mentality.

Our Role in Helping Kids Learn to Trust Christ

In life and in faith, growth is a process. Our job as parents throughout this process is twofold: First, we help our kids learn to trust God and create the kind of environment where they are able to explore faith and trust while practicing their freedom to respond in love. Second, we model an unconditional, nonjudgmental, and ever-embracing love in which our kids can do nothing that jeopardizes or even lessens that love.

But I'll be the first to admit that this is easier said than done.

An issue that seems rather minor now, but surely wasn't when our boys were in middle school, was our boys' wearing their baseball hats in church. The battles tended to be more about who would win (us or our sons) than about hats in church. Inevitably, we as parents won, but not without having to pull the parental power card. Usually I waited until we got in the van to mention the hats, without warning or process. They in turn, predictably, would grouse and argue.

Finally, when our boys were eleven and fourteen, we had a series of conversations about why they wanted to wear a hat in church and why we didn't think it was respectful. After that we made progress. (It actually didn't bother us much, but there were several folks, especially older folks, in our church who were clearly and vocally bothered by the hats.) Helping them see that the hats were not really the issue at all, but how we were called to treat people, even if we disagreed with them, was what ultimately mattered.

Dee and I were trying to help our boys put their own desires aside and to trust that Jesus would in time help adults at church understand that to a middle school guy, wearing a hat was vital to his social survival (at the time) and not a matter of disrespect. We eventually did get to the place where our boys agreed to forgo their hats for the sake of others who were bothered by their hats. So even if the adults were more concerned with their sense of propriety and decorum than whether an eighth grader wanted to be in church at all, our guys came to own the decision to hold off on the hats in church. (But the second they were on the patio, forget it!)

Sticky Faith Made Practical

The all-important question, then, that puts wheels on the biblical call to trust God to change us from the inside out is, "What does it mean to trust God?" or to put it another way, "How do we put this into practice every day?" We suggest three ways to help foster this kind of faith: teach your kids that obedience is our response to trusting God, frame all family discussions and activities as opportunities to know and trust Christ, and respond with grace when your child misbehaves.

Focus on Trusting God versus Obeying God

With apologies to the old hymn "Trust and Obey," theologically trusting God and obeying God are not meant to be seen as two equal and different tasks of the Christian life. Trusting God is the call of the gospel, as we've seen in Galatians 5. Obedience, then, is our response as we trust. In other words, God makes it clear that he is not interested in obedience geared merely to obtain his favor, yet obeying him is important.

Imagine your daughter is the target of vengeful gossip. Our default parenting style might be to offer a quick fix by tossing out a bumper-sticker platitude, perhaps quoting 2 Timothy 2:24, "And the Lord's servant must not be quarrelsome but must be kind to everyone." Then we might follow that up with, "Honey, God wants you to be kind to people, so you need to forgive her and move on." Done. End of story.

This kind of "obey God, move on" Christian parenting may or may not be helpful in the immediate situation, but in the long term it is certainly counterproductive to Sticky Faith. Instead, use this event to reinforce the idea of trusting Christ in ordinary life circumstances. First, assure your daughter that the Lord understands what she is going through and has been there. Following that, remind her that Christ can be trusted even when others cannot, and that the Lord has promised to be with her and protect her. Then, as you talk about trusting God, who is faithful and powerful, she may be given the ability to be kind to that person.

When we take the time to help our kids respond to their circumstances with love from the standpoint of trusting Jesus with their struggles, instead of offering quick and directive advice, we point them toward Sticky Faith. This builds in them a willingness to live out of an obedience that is based on knowing and walking with God, as opposed to "be nice, God says so."

Frame Discussions and Activities as Opportunities to Know and Trust Christ

Too often we talk about the everyday issues of life in a way that leaves Christ in the corner of the room, or even outside, until it's time to have the "God talk" around the table. For many, family devotions are genuine, sincere, and enjoyable times to focus on God together. Especially when kids are younger, family devotions can be a useful tool to help them see God as an active member of the family.

As kids get older, family devotions can sometimes become exercises that are more about getting through the ritual than a way to encourage our kids to talk about God as a family. When kids reach middle school or so, the most productive kinds of family devotions are often those that are less rigid and scheduled, and more organic and even spontaneous (what we sometimes in our family call "planned spontaneity"). These kinds of "God talks" can provide opportunities to integrate faith and the Lord into our normal conversation, instead of falling into a forced, and maybe even boring or "religious," production.

If you're talking with your son or daughter and you can tell they are giving you the Sunday school answers they think you want to hear, push them a bit deeper by asking "Why?" or "What makes you say that?" Take the time to dig a bit deeper in your conversation to unearth your child's authentic thoughts and feelings.

When discussing whether a film is appropriate for a teenager to see, for instance, perhaps steer the question not to WWJD but to "What does it mean to trust Jesus with how I spend my money?" or "As we trust Jesus for our entertainment and fun, how does that change how we make our weekend plans?" Parents have to be creative and, again, organic and contextual in bringing ordinary issues and

I understand and seek for my walk with Christ to be much more holistic than it ever was in high school. God calls me into a relationship with him, which then calls into play every area of my life. As a follower of Jesus, my faith is more than a youth group event or a "quiet time." (Oh, how I hate that term!) It affects the way I spend my money, the way I spend my time, the career path I choose, the way I treat my body, the way I treat the environment.... These things have the potential to be my spiritual act of worship. And as I seek a more holistic Christian faith, the more united I feel with Jesus' call and vision for the world, and the more fulfilled I feel spiritually.

—Sophie

faith together. Over time, especially with the bigger issues, this helps our children see that trust in Jesus, and how that trust is eventually translated into love, is the only thing that counts to God.

When we were invited to move from Denver to teach at Fuller Seminary in Pasadena, we decided to include our kids in the conversation. The process was far from perfect, and in thinking back, there are things we might have done differently. But the one thing we are glad we did was to let them know that their voices mattered as we tried to decide what God was saying to us as a family.

During that season of processing whether God was calling us to move, we spent several long dinners discussing the pros and cons of moving from the "home of the Broncos" to the wild metroplex of Southern California. Dee and I took the lead in steering the discussion to the question of God's desire and design for us, and what it would look like to trust the Lord with this decision. As we look back, we sometimes wonder what God was up to with this move. But this outcome we have seen: all three of our children, now in their twenties, approach life as a grand adventure of trust and risk. Each is walking their own faith journey; they are at various stages, but all three would tell anyone who asked that there is no other way to live.

To further illustrate, here are a few sample topics that families deal with every day. These tips and ideas are offered only to prime the pump of your own ideas. Don't feel like you have to try them all right now. Given your family's personality and schedule, choose a few to experiment with over the next month to grow together in trusting God.

Trust God with Your Money

As a family, adopt a Compassion or World Vision child and write monthly letters to them.

Schedule a "family giving meeting," in which every child and adult has equal say in how the family is going to distribute the funds the family has available, or even those funds that require sacrifice so another family has clothes at Christmas. (Notice I didn't say tithing, because some of us have lots more than 10 percent to give to those in need, and that is one more way to teach our children that we no longer live by rules or laws. In freedom, we give freely as God has given to us.)

Build into your family life regular patterns that remind you that all of your money belongs to God. Every Christmas, our family begins the morning by reading Luke 2, praying, and then deciding where our "Christmas gift" will go for the year. Each year, one family member gets to suggest to which charity the gift goes, and how much, and then we discuss it until we come to consensus.

Teach your children to be extravagant with the resources God has entrusted to them. For example, when you go out to eat, represent Christ to the person who serves you. When appropriate, let the waiter or waitress see or discover that you are a Christ-following family by asking them when you pray if there is anything they need prayer for. Because most waitstaff have experienced Christians as among the rudest people and worst tippers they serve, give them a far bigger tip than they would likely receive from anyone else, regardless of the level of service. Generosity to all, not only to those in need but toward everyone, is an expression of God's graciousness to us, and it helps us to trust him even more.[2]

Trust God with Your Time

As a family, take on one service project in the community a month.

As a family, do something together for the church at least monthly.

As a family, or at least with one of your children, teach a Sunday school class or children's summer program.

Take one day a month or quarter to play with your child. I have heard it said to "never let your child's education get in the way of your child's education," meaning sometimes a day with you at the beach or a movie and lunch will have more long-term impact than sitting in class for that one day.

Make the dinner experience a sacred time and space. At least once a week, gather everybody in the kitchen a half hour before dinner until a half hour after dinner. No phone calls, no checking texts or emails, and no TV. Everybody finishes the preparation, everybody serves each other, and everyone helps clean up. Play a game. Sing a song. Dance.

Trust God with Your Relationships

Invite another family, or those who need some family time, to eat a meal once a month or more.

Open your home and family to your neighbors and friends from work, church, or school.

On special holidays, have an open house for those who have no place else to go.

Adopt a senior adult or couple to be additional, or surrogate, grandparents.

Invite others into your lifestyle, plans, and major decisions. Have a small group that is as committed to you as a family as they are to the adults in the small group. Raise each other's kids. (More on this in chapter 5.)

Respond with Grace
When Your Child Misbehaves

Because our kids grow up in an increasingly complex and precarious world, filled with expectations and agendas that at times feel impossible to navigate, the odds are great that your child will "cross the line," or for some of our kids, catapult over the line. What do we do then?

Default with compassion. When our kids go through rough spots, whether it is because of circumstances beyond their control or the choices they make, their greatest need from us is gentle stability and compassion. Regardless of the offense, whether getting a D or getting arrested, underneath the rhetoric and even outright outbursts, your child is not doing this to get at you. Even in the most egregious of situations, remember that they are, at the core, suffering, and they need you to care. As Jesus cares for us in all we go through, so we too are dispensers of his grace.

Don't panic. There are very few issues you will face as parents that are irredeemable, even the biggies. Regardless of the circumstance, becoming overly distraught or emotional, especially within earshot (or eyeshot) of your child, only heightens your child's sense of dread, fear, and shame. We can take Paul's words seriously: "Don't fret or worry. Instead of worrying, pray. Let petitions and praises shape your worries into prayers, letting God know your concerns. Before you know it, a sense of God's wholeness, everything coming together for good, will come and settle you down. It's wonderful what happens when

Christ displaces worry at the center of your life"
(Phil. 4:6–7 MSG).

Take the long view. The ultimate hope that is part and
parcel of trusting God is the hope we have that in the
long run, God's mercy will win. We may not see it or
experience it exactly the way we want to for months,
or even years, but trusting Christ means we believe
that he is at work, bringing healing and redemption
to the most hopeless of circumstances. Parenting is
a marathon, but in Christ, as we trust him, we are
offered the gift of hope.

A Few Final Notes

In this chapter, we make the distinction between a performance-driven gospel of sin management and a Sticky Faith
of trusting Jesus to lead, guide, and change us from the
inside out. In making the case, we do not claim that trusting Jesus with our lives is easily understood. There is a great
deal of mystery involved in how God works with and in us
by the Holy Spirit. We sometimes can barely figure this out
for ourselves, much less teach it to our children. We need
God to help us know how to put this together. And in this
truth lies our hope.

The greatest gift you can give your children is to let them
see you struggle and wrestle with how to live a lifetime of
trust in God. As you live out your faith in trust, your life will
never be static, stale, or boring. You will be disappointed,
discouraged, and maybe even thrown around a bit at times.
You likely will even wonder if such a life is really worth it.
But as you faithfully hold on to the God who has taken hold
of you, the life you live and model will be a beacon of hope

and direction that no sin-management faith can hope to achieve. As you trust the gospel, and the Lord who saves, your Sticky Faith will help your children discover their own Sticky Faith.

sticky reflection and discussion questions

1. Dallas Willard describes the "gospel of sin management" as dealing only with sin and its effects, instead of the real life we live. In what ways is your faith an experience of the gospel of sin management?

2. What is the biggest obstacle to helping your son or daughter understand that the primary call of the Christian is to trust Christ? Describe where this is a difficult concept for you, and where it lines up with what you already believe and practice.

3. We stated that "obedience is the response to trust." Why is it better to begin with trust and then respond through obedience? Is it ever good to go the other direction: obey first and hope that trust follows? Have you ever experienced either of these in your faith journey? If so, what was it like, and what happened?

4. How do you see your child's faith in light of this chapter? Where do you see them growing in what it means to trust Christ, and where do you see them living out of the do's and don'ts of Christianity?

sticky identity

*I heard someone say "the fence is down," and by that
they meant the fence of your school, your family, your
church, your friends, who were once a fence around
you, saying, "This is the type of person that you are,"
or "This is what you are and are not allowed to do,"
or "This is what is and is not appropriate."
That fence drops way down as soon as you get to
college, and I saw that instantly. First day on campus,
your parents drive away, no one knows you....
Suddenly I was faced with this situation in which
I could literally have recreated myself in some ways
if I wanted to, and nobody would have known
that I had ever been any different.*
—Emily

*When I started college I was the person that my parents
wanted me to be. Now I feel like I found myself.*
—Max

In the summer of 2010, MTV launched a reality show called
If You Really Knew Me. The producers traveled to high schools
around the country and gave kids a chance to expose the

"real me" to each other and the world. Episode after episode, "normal" kids—jocks, nerds, beauty queens, class clowns, the gamut of stereotyped adolescents—revealed to the cameras that who they are on the outside is not who they really are. The most intriguing part of the show was how every kid was desperate to integrate and reconcile the "real me" with the "outside me" they lived at school. It's not that the kids didn't know who they were; it's that they had lots of "real me's."

In its efforts to captivate its adolescent viewers, MTV devoted this show to one of the most pressing questions your child will ask growing up: "Who am I?" This question haunts every teenager, especially during high school and early college.

In my (Chap's) work studying kids, I've received hundreds of notes, poems, letters, and songs expressing what adolescents think and feel. The majority of these notes reflect students' attempts to understand who they are, and who they want and sometimes need to be. As one note put it, "Everybody knows who I am, and they tell me all the time. My mom knows I'm a 'good kid.' My dad says I am lazy but a natural athlete. My teachers tell me I'm smart, but I don't care enough to 'live up to my potential.' My friends think I'm funny. Girls think I'm shy. I think I'm all of those … and none of those. Who the heck am I? I'm everything to everybody, and nobody to me."

Your sons and daughters don't consciously ask themselves, "Who am I going to be today?" Typically, when they travel from class to lunch to sports to friends to church, they subconsciously know that they have to produce a self that fits the needs and expectations of others in that setting.

Their school self can be very different from their church self, which is often diametrically opposed to their friends self.

This pressure to live out a self that may or may not align with their other selves is at the very least exhausting, and it can at times be painful. Most parents hear at one time or another from their frustrated adolescent, "You don't even *know* me!" Our kids don't yet know themselves, yet they desperately want to be known. They want to know their personality, their gifts and skills and interests. They want to know where they came from and where they're going. They want to know where they belong, in what group or city or career or intimate relationship. They want to know what they believe and how that affects their life. In short, they're struggling to form their identity.

As your children grow up, who they are will evolve and take many different expressions. In that process, we as parents can help instill Sticky Faith by modeling for and reminding our children that their ultimate sense of themselves is best found in the Lord's answer to the pressing "Who am I?" question. But first let's look at the arduous process of identity formation.

Sticky Findings

Identity Formation Is Affected by Brain Development

The process of forming an identity takes years. Although there are some similarities between early adolescents (who are between ten or eleven years old and fourteen) and late adolescents (who are approximately fourteen to twenty years old), there is a significant difference in how they think about their identity.[1] We now know that the brain functions with the concreteness of a child throughout early adolescence and begins the abstraction of adulthood at around age fourteen (thus making the shift from early to late adolescence). In other words, while your abstract sixteen-year-old will be able to pull together a variety of experiences to figure out how they are going to handle a contentious teacher, your concrete twelve-year-old will barely be able to remember they had math that morning.

Years ago researchers believed that social and cognitive maturity was reached in the early twenties and even late teens. Today's academic community generally agrees that developmental life has changed so dramatically over the last few decades that it now takes young people into the mid to late twenties to begin to settle as adults. We now have physical evidence, for example, that cognitive maturity is increasing: MRI studies reveal that it takes ten years, from roughly ages fifteen to twenty-five, for the brain to complete the process and arrive at full physiological adulthood.[2]

Social scientists tend to believe that this lengthy process of brain development has changed over time. In centuries past across cultures, the shift from child to adult took much less time. (Adolescence, in fact, is a relatively new phase of development, arriving just over a hundred years ago.) We now know that the process of discovering and living out an integrated personal identity, or a sense of self that drives decisions, morality, and life choices, takes longer than it did even thirty years ago.[3]

For us as parents, our high school graduation was the opportunity to put into practice our emerging self—our ideas, dreams, and plans. In comparison, many of today's midtwenties college graduates have a hard time deciding what they want to do, much less who they are. In terms of identity and adult independence, today's twenty-three-year-old is often the developmental equivalent of a seventeen-year-old in 1980. Few scholars debate this point, yet society and, in response, human development are changing so rapidly—from the impact of technology to the rapidly diminishing sense of meaningful community—that researchers are scrambling to keep up. Parents need to keep in mind that the world our kids are growing up in is far different from the world in which we grew up, and that changes everything for them.

For additional resources about identity development, visit *www.stickyfaith.org*.

Identity Formation Is a Long and Winding Process

In early adolescence, because thinking is still childlike and concrete, your child will not spend much time reflecting on her personal identity. Your middle schooler might, by his behavior and attitudes, intuitively ask "Who am I?" but he is not yet aware that this is what he is doing. At this stage, your child's biggest needs are to be affirmed and surrounded by safe and loving adults and to have his choices and life protected by appropriate boundaries.

Right around ninth grade, as the brain begins to shift from concrete to abstract thinking and awareness, your child will show expressions of adult commitment and fleshed-out identity. Be warned, however, that you will likely also see plenty of immature behavior. This is one of the more confusing aspects of parenting adolescents today: sometimes your kid will astound you with adultlike maturity, and simultaneously he will surprise you with an attitude or behavior that demonstrates the exact opposite. I have seen my own kids go through several iterations of identity achievement, only to bounce back through the process when another crisis hits. Whether it's dealing with employers or coaches, handling money, or believing that if parking tickets are ignored they will eventually go away, in today's complex and precarious world, the process of developing a strong, integrated identity is a long and winding process. As parents, our job is to know that all of this conflicting, inconsistent, and confusing behavior is actually our kids' way of discovering who they are and making the commitments toward who they want to be.

Students Often Shelve
Their Faith for a Time

In his interviews with 125 students as they transitioned from high school to college, sociologist Tim Clydesdale discovered that most college freshmen are overwhelmed by what he called "daily life management" — managing school and social networks (friends, authority figures, romantic partners).[4] Clydesdale observes that rather than diving into figuring out who they are, students store away important parts of themselves (often including, but not limited to, their spiritual identity) in an "identity lockbox" when they enter college. College life is simply a series of disconnected events —without linkage to one's true self and without regard to previous commitments, including faith.[5] Although Clydesdale's study was focused primarily on the transition from high school to college, a similar observation could apply to older high school kids as well.

Several of the students interviewed by the Fuller Youth Institute acknowledged that they put their faith on hold when they entered college so that they could "enjoy the college life." Translated, that means *party*. And yet when asked about shelving their faith, a couple of them noted the inconsistency of it all. "I know it doesn't make sense. If I kick God to the curb for four years just so I can have fun, then why would I pick him up again? Obviously I don't think he's worthwhile, or I wouldn't dog him in the first place. I mean, we are talking about God, right?" Right.

> *I think that I don't have time to go to church anymore because I'm usually busy. But it's still in the back of my head. I just don't have time to actually go to church.*
> —Gabbi

Because we are looking for consistency and growth, if and when we see our kids shelving their faith, we can feel like we are losing them. But we have to remember that identity and faith formation is a messy process of "two steps forward, one step back." In fact, my children, now in their twenties, have not quite completed their adolescent-to-adulthood stories. Yes, each one has achieved certain levels of commitment with various aspects of their identity. But at the same time, life circumstances and growing up in today's culture can throw off—for a season or longer—their strongly held identity commitments.

Sometimes this is disheartening for us as parents, but overall our commitment has been to hold fast to the truth that each of their stories is unique.

Parenting is not for the faint of heart or for those who like fast food over the real thing. Often what we see is encouraging and even exhilarating, but there are those times when our children's journeys are rocky and slippery, and we so desperately want to jump in and treat them like ten-year-olds. When you get to this season, the best you can do for your child is to be available and consistent. (We'll unpack this more in chapter 8.)

Sticky Faith Made Practical

By now you might be wondering what identity development has to do with a book on Sticky Faith.

Everything, because who we are as people, and how we grow up acting based on our sense of who we are, is directly connected to our faith journey. To help our children develop Sticky Faith, it is our job first to understand their process of trying to discover who they are, and then to create the environment that supports this discovery and commitment process.

Remember Your Child
Is God's Beloved Creation

Henri J. M. Nouwen, well-loved spirituality writer and pastoral-counseling professor, wrote extensively on the spirituality of identity. During a small retreat we were privileged to attend, Nouwen mused that every person is hounded by a single question throughout their lives: "Who am I?" On a small whiteboard he listed the three ways we seek to answer that question:

> "I am what I do."
>
> "I am what I control."
>
> "I am what others say about me."

Each of these responses is inadequate, and even destructive, for both us and our kids. If I'm honest as a father, our kids' performance (what they did and how well they did it) and how we, and others, described them shaped their sense of self. It is not that doing well, or being accomplished, is a bad thing. But when how well our kids do at something becomes the primary rubric for discovering who they are, we do them no favors.

To Nouwen, the answer to the single most important question affecting all of humanity, "Who am I?" is the message of Jesus and the Bible.[6] Your child has been created, redeemed, and called to live as God's precious and beloved child.

Your son may be good at many things and bring you great joy as his personality develops. Your daughter may show such amazing promise as you watch her grow into a young woman with much to offer the world. But beneath all of their gifts and talents and abilities, each and every child is more than the sum of their abilities and personality. At their core, each is the beloved child of God.

My wife and I first encountered Nouwen's writing when our children were still quite young—ten, seven, and four years old. From that time on, we have done our best to remind ourselves and our kids that each of them is a profound gift from God, and we are his somewhat flawed dispensers of grace to them.[7]

Treat Each Child as an Individual

Each of our kids, like yours, is different. One loved soccer growing up, and one gave it a shot for a while but quickly moved on to other sports. One loved to dance, and another wanted to be a musician. For a season, one struggled with a temporary learning disability, another showed signs of brilliance as a child, while another was just a naturally good student.

One got in trouble—a lot. Another got in trouble some but was harder on himself than we could ever be, and another was a bit of a pleaser who wanted peace above all. One sulked and retreated when sad, another would wander off and stare at the sky for hours, and another silently stayed close. One got mad at the drop of a hat, another avoided conflict and got defensive, and the other took a while learning to speak up. They're all funny. Really.

Today, one's faith is a straightforward journey of commitment and service, another is settling into the arms of the Lord, and another sees life differently but "still holds on to Jesus."

Who are our kids? We ask that question often. And yet we know the answer. None of our kids are defined by what they do, what they control, what they're good at, or most of the time by what others say (as hard as that last one is). Each child is a beloved individual, created and known by God himself.

Use Your Community to Develop Personal Identity

The concept of identity includes both a personal dimension, as in "who I see myself to be as distinct from others," and a communal dimension, as in "who I am as connected to others." Our culture too often focuses only on our own sense of self, as in who *I* want to be. In building a biblical Sticky Faith, who I seek to be has to be bigger than just me and my dreams. A rich and sustainable faith recognizes that as I walk in community with God's people, I ultimately discover who I am.

Even before we had kids, Dee and I committed with a handful of friends to walk through life together. This has been an important and life-giving aspect of our journey for the past thirty-plus years. Whatever small group we have been part of, we always invited the kids of those in the group to feel as though it was their group as well.

When one of the kids in our group was in a play, for example, we all attended. When there was a birthday, we at least sent an email or called, if not gave a small gift. When a daughter of one of our group got married, all the guys felt like we were giving her away. (Luckily we didn't have to help pay for it, but we would have!) One of our kids is in parachurch ministry raising his own support, and those friends are his biggest supporters. But more important, they are his biggest fans as well.

You can build a Christian community around your kids in a number of ways. Some families have extended family who live nearby, and for many, they provide great support and strength for kids. Or perhaps you are part of a school, which may be faith-based or public, or a neighborhood organization. Your church and your friendships can also offer nourishing ties. The point is to build "social capital" into your child's life, creating a network of caring believers who will pray for, mentor, and bless your children with their presence over the course of their lives. (More on this in chapter 5, "A Sticky Web of Relationships.")

Finally, do your children a favor and explore with them how their family—in both its environment and genetics —has shaped them. Make a family tree. Explore how your ethnic and religious backgrounds have shaped who you are. Talk about your personality traits and interests and how you are the same as or different from other families. Celebrate your family's positive traits and point out its problems. But do not stop there: make it your aim to invite your children as they grow up to appropriately wrestle with how both their extended as well as their nuclear families may struggle. The more open you are to exploring your personal and com-munal identity, and encourage honesty and dialogue about issues that may at times be painful, the more your child will have the vocabulary and framework for developing her own identity.

Use Rituals to Reinforce Identity

Having your son or daughter's identity centered fundamen-tally on being God's child may feel theoretical or "spiritual" to the point of meaninglessness—for your kids and maybe for you too. Simply telling your child that she is a beautiful gift who is cherished and talented may not make much of a difference when she is faced with the messages (some good, most not so good) that confront her every day. Getting the myths and lies of who she is off center stage requires more robust communication and experiences.

Enter rituals.

A ritual may sound like some ancient or unusual practice,

like chanting by candlelight. But a ritual is simply a social custom, or even a normal way of going about something, that provides the comfort of history, regularity, and even tradition. How you celebrate Christmas, for example, is filled with rituals. What happens when you eat together, prepare for a big event, or visit relatives often has elements of ritual that help remind everyone that you are a community that has its own rules, norms, and customs.

Healthy rituals can include both daily activities and yearly celebrations. Here are some ways to incorporate rituals into your family life.

After school, at dinner, or at bedtime, spend a few minutes debriefing your child's day. Focus the conversation on how they felt about the day, where they felt like they could be themselves, and what held them back from doing so at other times.

Celebrate every birthday, anniversary, first day of school, first day of Notre Dame football—whenever you can find an excuse to celebrate—way beyond what is "reasonable." Decorate with abandon: candles, streamers, balloons, posters. Find a favorite food that matches the celebration. (For us it's a 6:00 a.m. Swedish pancake feast for birthdays, and for big sporting events or fun movies, it's fondue.)

At every birthday, when you pray for the gathered meal, have each person pray a word of thanksgiving for the unique gift of the one whose birthday it is. Follow up with a specific blessing that appropriately affirms that person's character and place in the family.

Make it a habit to tuck your child in bed, even through middle school (if they'll let you). As you kiss them good night, pray with and for your child. In your prayer, thank the Lord that you have been given God's child to know and love. As they get older, invite them into your room to pray together.

> To get even more ideas about rituals you can try with your children, visit *www.stickyfaith.org*.

Help Your Child Grow through Hardship

As parents, the last thing we want is for our kids to experience pain. But as Paul writes in Romans 5:3–4, "Suffering produces perseverance; perseverance, character; and character, hope." I wish it weren't this way, but suffering is one of God's primary avenues of growth and identity formation.

We can help our sons and daughters by looking out for particular "trigger" events that could create crises that lead to growth, such as the loss of a loved one, an argument with a friend, or difficulty in school. Of course, not all difficulties are major (or seem major to us as adults); some are comparatively minor, such as new questions about their faith, new patterns of minor misbehavior, or an overburdened schedule. Any experience your child has with the stresses and strains of life can be valuable in helping them wrestle more deeply with who God has made them.

Our kids grow not when we stand as goalies preventing pain from entering the net of their lives but when we are present and listen carefully when they feel beat up, confused, and defeated.

Research points to the importance, in addition to listening well, of both supporting and challenging our children to create the optimal environment for growth. Harvard developmental psychologist Robert Kegan sums this up well: "People grow best when they continuously experience an ingenious blend of support and challenge; the rest is commentary. Environments that are weighted too heavily in the direction of challenge are toxic. They promote defensiveness and constriction. Those weighted too heavily toward support are ultimately boring; they promote devitalization … [T]he balance of challenge and support leads to vital engagement."[8]

Having the support of caring parents who do not hide pain or struggle from their kids can help kids navigate the heartache and hardship of life in a broken world. This may at times feel uncomfortable or risky, as when we wrestle with the reality of cancer or discuss an unfair or vindictive teacher. But we must engage our kids in honest conversation and dialogue, soliciting their opinion and voice, especially during those times of struggle. If you are honest and open with any issue of life or faith, your child will be a much better thinker, not to mention theologian.

Use Extracurricular Activities to Explore Identity

Too often we as parents use extracurricular activities such as sports or music to focus on finding or developing a particular skill. However, we should celebrate who our kids are in the midst of their involvement more than, or at least as much as, their accomplishment and skill. I used to buy milkshakes for a goal scored, until our late-bloomer second child said driving home after another goalless afternoon, "I guess I'll never get a milkshake, huh, Dad?"

Every child needs to be encouraged and to know that they are valuable and have unique contributions to offer. With sports, we tend to value only those things that are immediately measured — goals scored, tackles made, and so on. But congratulating them for the little things, like listening well to the coach, practicing at home, and being a friend to other kids regardless of where they are on the "star scale," will help your child see that the deeper character issues are more important.

Focus on personal goals by helping your child define their success by their commitment and effort. The key is to make sure *their* goals are being pursued, as opposed to our goals. I have talked to scores of high school kids who still resent their parents' pushing them incessantly to reach "their potential," when the kids just wanted to have fun with their friends.

Model and teach character, like love of enemy (or opponent), suffering for the best of others, and letting others get credit and opportunities before you.

Use the social relationships that develop through sports or activities to come alongside other families to love and serve them.

Treat each sport, or any other activity, as an opportunity to use our gifts, passions, talents, and relationships for God's kingdom purposes.

Affirm Character Growth More Than Academic Achievement

As with sports, celebrate and affirm character development above academic achievement (like modeling and teaching respect for others, especially adults and those peers that others shun).

Create an atmosphere that views academic achievement as a gift to see what God has in store for your child, as opposed to disconnected from "real world" requirements. Approach homework, tests, and papers as encouraging and empowering ways to explore how God has wired your child.

Every semester, set realistic academic goals with your child, and negotiate a plan that you both feel good about (including time for homework versus the computer or TV, weekly goals, monthly goals, etc.). Every week check in and evaluate what's working and what's not. When they struggle, alter the plan—hire a tutor, set up a study group, do "adult" homework beside them while they do their homework.

As a steward of God's beloved child, help your kid do what is so hard for most of us adults: find balance in their life. In the midst of the demands and agendas of schoolwork, activities, general busyness, and church, walk closely with your child in making time for what matters. Most of us fill the calendar activity by activity instead of proactively, well in advance, making decisions that ensure the best for the family and each child. Your goal is to train your kid to see life as a whole, connected adventure, versus a frantic race from one expectation and agenda to another.

Model a Relationship with God

Model for your child that, more than just a worldview or a way of life, Christianity is first and foremost an intimate relationship with the Father. Remind her that in the end, you as parents are also fellow children of God, and therefore God is the Father of the entire family.

Discuss, consider, and make all decisions based on what it means to live the life of the beloved—including money, politics, friendships, and how you treat your neighbor.

When your child fails or is disappointed, model a tenderness that communicates that God understands and will in time lift them up. Living as God's beloved child does not mean that pain and suffering won't come, but through gentle encouragement, they can know God has a purpose and a trajectory for them that is unique and good.

A Few Final Notes

The hardest part about writing a book like this, especially when it comes to such a long and arduous process as identity formation, is how much mystery is involved. There are no formulas for our sons and daughters' deciding and discovering who they ultimately want to be. Being a parent today is in turns challenging, intimidating, and invigorating.

Sticky Faith is not a faith that avoids struggle or even dormant seasons. Sticky Faith is giving our kids the very best we have to offer as they pursue who they are as a person, in community and in Christ. Our kids are each a unique masterpiece created by the mighty hand of God. Each one is the beloved of God and is therefore called to belong to and serve this King as long as they have breath. Regardless of how they act, struggle, or make us proud, this is who they are, each one: the beloved child of God.

sticky reflection and discussion questions

1. What are some ways you defined yourself growing up? How were they helpful to you as you grew older? How were they harmful?

2. Of Nouwen's three answers to the question "Who am I?" which of these are you most prone to rely on? Describe what that looks and feels like. Which of these does your child rely on? What does that look like?

3. On a scale of 1 to 7, 1 being easy, 7 not so easy, how hard is it for you to see yourself as the beloved child of God? How easy is it for your child? Describe what you mean.

4. Name some ways you can emphasize who your child is (a beloved child of God) rather than what your child does. How would this emphasis change your approach to your child's extracurricular activities or academic achievements?

sticky faith conversations

My mom has been sick most of my life, but I've seen the strength of her faith, her love for the Lord, and her trust that he is in control and will give her the strength she needs each day. Just watching that has influenced me in amazing ways.
—Selena

Even though my mother was actually working at the church for a while as the music minister . . . we didn't talk about faith at home. Still don't talk about it at home.
—Anthony

Imagine we planted a microphone in your house.

Scary. We know.

And imagine we recorded a week's worth of your family's conversations.

What would be the number one topic of discussion? I'm guessing it would be logistics, like your daughter asking you to take her to the art store for supplies to finish her class project and your son asking when his friend can come over to shoot some hoops.

What percent of your conversations would explicitly mention God, or have an overt connection to your faith? What's your guess?

How do you feel about your answer?

On the one hand, there are those of us who clam up when it comes to discussions that might involve mentions of God or faith. On the other hand, there are those of us who gush, maybe to the point of annoying and alienating our sons or daughters. In between these extremes, how do you find the middle ground of authentic and organic conversations about faith?

Typically when I (Kara) talk with parents about the fruit that comes from discussing matters of faith as a family, a parent will chime in that they believe in living out their faith in front of their kids instead of merely talking about it.

As we said in the early pages of this book, who you are as a parent is far more important than what you say. If I had to choose between living out my faith or talking about my faith in front of my kids, I'd choose the former every time.

But I don't have to choose. And neither do you. We can do both.

While we know that actions speak louder than words, words still really matter. So how can you make sure that you create both a tone and a schedule that encourage conversations that further Sticky Faith? Far more important than any microphone we would plant (don't worry, we don't know where you live), your kids are listening and learning from the way you talk—or don't talk—about faith.

Sticky Findings

Most Parents Don't Talk about Faith with Their Kids

At Fuller Seminary, we have great respect and affection for the Search Institute, a fellow research center devoted to helping families, schools, and kids make the world a better place for kids. According to the Search Institute's nationwide study of 11,000 teenagers from 561 congregations across six denominations, 12 percent of youth have a regular dialogue with their mom on faith or life issues.[1] In other words, just one out of eight kids talks with their mom about their faith.

It's far lower for dads. One out of twenty kids, or 5 percent, has regular faith or life conversations with their dad.

One additional interesting statistic: approximately 9 percent of teenagers engage in regular reading of the Bible and devotions with their families. So not even one out of ten teenagers looks at Scripture with their parents. When it comes to matters of faith, mum's usually the word at home.

Students Whose Parents Talk about Faith Have More Sticky Faith

The relatively small group of parents who do talk with their kids about faith tend to default to asking their kids questions:

> What did you talk about in church today?
>
> How was youth group?
>
> What did you think of the sermon?

Depending on the personality and mood of your kid, responses usually range from grunts to "the usual." Not very satisfying for you or your kid.

71

Our research shows that asking questions can pay off. But as vital to Sticky Faith is that you also share about your own faith. In other words, don't just interview your kids; discuss your own faith journey and all of its ups and downs too.

Christian Parents Tend to Avoid Tricky Subjects

Part of why students stay silent is because the adults in their lives don't know how (or maybe are afraid or too busy) to talk about tricky subjects. It's almost like we have a parental list of topics to avoid with our kids.

Sex is certainly on that list. Two different sets of data indicate that the more important religion (not just Christianity but also other religions) is to parents, the more difficult it is for those same parents to talk with their kids about sex.[2]

I find that incredibly ironic. We as followers of Christ should be at the front of the line to talk with our kids about sex because we know that sex, when done right, is a fantastic gift from God. Somehow with sex (and I would surmise with other controversial topics) our families have been robbed of healthy, balanced, scripturally guided conversations—the type of conversations that foster Sticky Faith.

Parents Who Talk about Doubts Help Build Sticky Faith

While it's often assumed that doubting our faith is wrong or even sinful, our research brings a counterperspective. At least in our study, students who feel the freedom and have opportunities to express their doubts tend to have more Sticky Faith.[3]

Unfortunately, students who are experiencing doubts

often stay silent. Less than half of the students in our survey share their doubts and struggles with adults or friends.

When we asked our students in college to reflect on the doubts they remembered having during high school, here is a sample of what they said (listed in random order):

> *My dad has always been somebody who I've been able to go to for theological questions and whenever I have doubts and issues and questions with what I'm reading in Scripture.*
>
> —Seoung

- If God would still love me if I had sex.

- If I was worth anything.

- If God really existed.

- If God was real and if he would forgive me for all the bad things I had done and was doing.

- Why God would allow terrible things to happen if he was so loving and sensitive.

- Why I feel like I am never able to hear God.

- If homosexuality is really such a bad thing.

- If non-Christians really go to hell, even if they are good people.

The answers above, as well as the rest of college kids' answers, tend to cluster into four categories:

1. Does God exist?
2. Does God love me?
3. Am I living the life God wants?
4. Is Christianity true or the only way to God?

These are good and honest questions. If our kids can't externally express these tough questions, they may internally fester and become toxic. Whether our kids' doubts are because of a postmodern skepticism of universal truth, a specific faculty member or student who directly questions the validity of Christianity, or their own valid questions about God and Scripture, our research shows that airing these questions in a safe, loving, affirming environment helps develop Sticky Faith.

Students with Sticky Faith Have Parents Who Encourage Individual Thought

A good faith conversation doesn't equal convincing your kid that what you believe is best. This probably doesn't surprise you, but your children don't want you to try to convince them to agree with you. Not only don't they want it, but they might reject your faith when you try.

Sticky Faith students often report that while their parents offered opinions, they ultimately gave the students some latitude to arrive at their own conclusions. As one student reported, "My parents have always been the kind of people who loved for me to learn on my own, to figure out life experiences on my own and to shape my own understanding of who God is.... You know one thing that I think is the most important in my relationships with my parents is ... that they have allowed us to learn and they have not made choices for us."

Sticky Faith Made Practical

With every topic in this book—whether it be the Sticky Gospel or a Sticky Faith identity or sticky church relationships—each family needs to figure out what works best for them. No two parents are alike, no two kids are alike, and no two families are alike. Throughout this book, we give you suggestions that you might copy or use as a springboard to come up with ideas that are even better for your family.

This is perhaps even more important when it comes to Sticky Faith discussions. Every family talks about life and faith differently.

I (Kara) saw this wonderful diversity one day when I had three different meetings with three different parents, all of whom were from the same church. Each parent had marvelous ideas about how to talk with their kids about faith, ideas that are included in this chapter. But none of the ideas overlapped. Each of these parents had the same destination in mind: healthy, honest conversations with their kids. But each had followed a different road map to get there, a road map that matched their family members' personalities and schedules.

So as you read—and especially after you walk away from —this chapter, have fun drawing your own map.

Provide Space and Time for Quality Conversations

I mentioned earlier that my own parenting is different every day because of our research. At the top of the long list of what I've learned is that my husband and I need to make the space and time for quality conversations.

Note I didn't say "hope" that space emerges.

I said we have to "make" the space.

In the midst of preparing dinner, writing emails, and thinking about tomorrow's meetings (usually all at once), it is so challenging to make time to really talk with my kids. I fail all the time. But when I fail, our research has made me more determined than ever to try, try again.

It helps our family to carve out time each week to be together—time we call "Powell Time." Sometimes the five of us stay together, but most of the time, Dave takes one or two of our kids and I take the other one or two. We mix it up each week so that both Dave and I get one-on-one (or one-on-two, since we have three kids) time with each of our kids. For our kids, one-on-one time is like gold.

Our goals in this time are twofold: to have fun and to talk. Usually it's cheap fun, like playing tennis or going on a hike or making cookies.

And then we sit and talk with each other, usually over frozen yogurt or fruit smoothies. We even have special notebooks for these conversations, notebooks our kids picked out for themselves at our first Powell Time. The parent starts the conversation, asking Nathan, Krista, or Jessica questions and capturing their answers in their journal.

Dave and I tend to ask questions like:

- What would your friends say they like about you?
- What do you wish was different about our family?
- Do you think our family is too busy, not busy enough, or just right?
- What's your idea of the best day ever?
- What do you like about your teacher these days?
- What do you wish were different?

Because of what we've learned about Sticky Faith, we next give our kids a chance to ask us questions, and we write down our answers. Their questions can be pretty amusing:

- What's your favorite dessert?
- What do you do all day at Fuller?
- What should we do during the next Powell Time?

Our kids are young, but we're trying to plant honest conversation into the DNA of our relationship.

Learn to Listen and Ask Questions, Not Lecture

Throughout our research process, parents have repeatedly told us that their best conversations with their kids occur in the midst of everyday life — when they are in the minivan together talking about soccer practice, or when their kid is stressed over finding a prom date. Those times of crisis or debriefings of the day's events are often the best springboards for deeper conversation.

While the timing of those conversations is based more on your kid's mood than anything else, you'll interact better with your son or daughter — whatever their mood or attitude — when you learn to listen and ask questions instead of lecture.

Let's be honest: parents lecturing kids hasn't worked.

Dallas Willard, who coined the phrase the "gospel of sin management," writes in the same book, "But now let us try a subversive thought. Suppose our failures occur, not in spite of what we are doing, but precisely because of it."[4] Maybe one of the main reasons we are struggling to communicate with our kids is that we are trying to communicate by lecturing.

One of the most important pieces of Sticky Faith communication advice we can share is this: never explain something to your kid if you can ask a question instead.

Why is this so important? Picture you and your child talking about premarital sex. Does your child know what you think about it? Does your child know what you would want to say to them about it? Odds are good that the answer to both questions is yes.

Because your child already knows what you think and what you would say, they will likely close their mind as soon as you open your mouth. One noted psychologist who is also a dad recently relayed the story of talking to his sixteen-year-old son about a behavior that the dad felt should be changed. After the dad's long and well-reasoned list of reasons the son should change, the son shrugged and said, "Are you done yet?" Note that the question was are *you* done yet, not are *we* done yet.

Create the Right Venue for Meaningful Conversation

During the course of our meetings with parents nationwide, our FYI team has been so impressed with their creativity in asking questions and creating venues for meaningful conversation. We've noticed that when children are younger, scheduled "dates" are quite effective; your kids will look forward to knowing when they get to go miniature golfing or on a hike with you.

As your children get older, perhaps around middle school, scheduled dates might seem less sincere. Your child might not appreciate it seeming like you had to schedule time with them to make it happen. Even if you do actually plan it ahead of time and enter it into your own schedule, you might not want them to know that. As your son or daughter enters adolescence, "planned spontaneity" is often more effective.

And we hope that planned spontaneity happens with both parents so that your son remains connected to his mom or stepmom, and your daughter gets quality time with her dad or stepdad.

A year ago I met Eileen, a mother of two teenagers who connects with her son and daughter by staying nearby when her kids have the TV on. If her kids are watching TV without her, she usually works in her nearby home office, keeping an ear tuned to words or phrases drifting from the TV room. When Eileen overhears a commercial or scene with sexual overtones, she'll ask questions like, "What do you think that ad was trying to say?" or "Why do you think they are using bikini-clad women to sell car wax?"

If her kids are watching a TV show with her, she's the one holding the remote. During or after scenes that show something sexual or related to drugs or alcohol—or anything controversial or provocative for that matter—Eileen will hit the pause button, ask her kids questions, and then often share her own thoughts.

Eileen has found that TV can be a great conversation starter on a variety of topics. She takes advantage of shows like *The Apprentice* and *The Office* to talk with her kids about appropriate office behavior. She'll ask her kids, "What should that character have done?"

I asked Eileen if her kids ever roll their eyes at her questions and commentary. "Sure, at times they do. But sometimes we get into good conversations. And every once in a while, they later parrot back to me something I've said. Like all parenting, I'm planting seeds."

A successful business leader I met focuses his conversational seed planting on one of his major values: wisdom. Many of his conversations with his three daughters revolve around helping them make better decisions. Often over dinner or as he's driving his girls to basketball practice, he talks to them about their day, keeping an ear tuned to the decisions they made throughout the day—decisions ranging from how they spent their time to how they interacted with friends. He asks them why they made the decisions they did, and if they would make the same decisions again. He shares with his girls both the good and not-so-good decisions he himself has made. He and his wife steer conversations in this direction because of their shared goal of teaching their girls to be independent thinkers.

Pouring effort, time, and thought into conversations with our kids doesn't end when they graduate from high school. Yesterday I spoke with Rowena, whose college-freshman son lives on campus at a university thirty minutes from their home. When Rowena calls his cell phone, he's often headed into class or on his way to lunch, so he never seems to have much time to talk. His occasional moodiness doesn't help.

But he does need regular haircuts. He likes the barber who cut his hair throughout high school, but he doesn't have a car at school to drive himself back home. So this busy mom of three makes the effort every month to pick up her son at school, take him for a haircut, and then drive him back.

At first her husband objected. "This is silly. He's a college student. He can get his own haircut."

But then Rowena explained that it wasn't about the haircut. It was about the thirty-minute car rides to and from the barber they had together—just the two of them. During the car rides she gets the best glimpse of how her son is doing; for instance, once he happened to mention that he had started attending Campus Crusade. He never would have mentioned that during their short phone calls, but the thirty-minute car rides give her son time to unpack his life.

Don't Avoid the Touchy Subjects

Whether it's in the car or somewhere else, bringing up tough subjects with our kids is never easy. When you're concerned about your teenager's actions, how do you talk with him or her in a way that provides some guidance and boundaries and yet fosters your kid's growing decision-making skills?

One of our colleagues at Fuller wrestled with this question when his seventeen-year-old son started swearing. A lot. This thoughtful dad asked his son, "Does your language match who you want to be as a follower of Jesus?" That simple question opened his son's eyes to the gap between who he wanted to be and how he was acting, and he decided to stop swearing.

> *Especially in high school, they were teaching me how to make good decisions. And kind of guiding me in that but really not controlling what I did as much as, "Let's talk through how to make a good godly decision and how you seek God's will for things."*
> —Annika

Even if you stumble and fail in your conversations about tough topics, it's worth it to keep trying. I met one dad who has decided to be as transparent as possible with his kids. His wife, Kathy, was raised in a family that talked about everything when she was young; everything, that is, except sex.

As Kathy grew older, she ended up feeling like she couldn't talk about a lot of other things with her mom. It was almost like the degree to which her mom felt comfortable talking about sex was the degree to which Kathy felt comfortable talking to her mom about other things. In some sort of conversational swimming pool, the depth to which Kathy's mom would go in a conversation about sex set the maximum depth for their overall relationship.

Even though I have messed up and will mess up, I want to go as deep as possible. Don't you?

> Free resources to help you have better conversations with your kids are available at *www.stickyfaith.org*.

Be Creative If Your Kid Doesn't Want to Talk to You

When I share with parents the importance of having good conversations with their kids, often one of them will sheepishly raise their hand and ask, "What do you do if your kid doesn't want to talk to you?"

Every teenager goes through seasons when they don't want to talk to their parents. What varies is the length and intensity of the season. The longer and more intense the season, the more creative we need to be as parents.

One mom desperately wanted to have meaningful conversations with her sixteen-year-old son, but he was uninterested. The last thing he wanted to do was spend time talking with her.

But he did love movies. So this proactive mom began scanning movie trailers, seeing which ones might be the most interesting to see with her son and hopefully talk about afterward. When those movies hit the theaters, she offered to take her son. He almost always accepted, and they usually had pretty good conversations on the drive home.

This mom found a way for conversations to seem organic and natural, even though she had actually devoted a fair amount of time to this plan. Remember, you are building toward a lifelong friendship, and faith is and will be an important part of that. Taking a walk, spontaneous shopping (especially for dads — a real winner!), coming home early for a bike ride, taking your kid to play pool or watch a few innings of their favorite baseball team — these are all ways to tell your son or daughter how important they are to you and that you value them as people.

Plus we can't assume that just because our kids say they don't want to talk to us, they really mean it. I'll never forget hearing the story of Jin, a pretty rough seventeen-year-old whose single dad sent her to a Christian school in hopes that it would "straighten her out." Whether it was because her friends were going or because she warmed up to "the whole God thing," Jin signed up for the school's spring break mission trip to Guatemala.

Jin ended up sitting on the flight next to Joe, the school's campus pastor. For the first few hours, Jin was her normal tough self. She put on her earphones and mostly ignored Joe. He tried to ask her questions about her family, but Jin summarized her relationship with her dad by saying, "I asked him to leave me alone. And he has."

Throughout the mission trip, the Lord worked in Jin and she softened. By the end of the trip, she confessed to Joe through her tears, "I wish my dad had not done what I asked. I wish he hadn't left me alone."

Jin, so do I.

Share Your Own Faith

As we've already noted, kids with Sticky Faith often have parents who share their own faith journeys with their kids. When you do share your experiences, please make sure you don't cross the line into parental lecturing. (Lots of parents miss that line, and believe me, your kids' alarm bells will go off when you cross it.)

Throughout this Sticky Faith research process, I've realized so many errors I've made as a parent. Take our family devotions. We try to have family devotions every weekend. At least in this season when our kids are in elementary school, family devotions give us a set time every week to focus on God together. Lest you be under any illusions, they last less than six minutes, and if it's an extra busy weekend or if there is a Chargers game, they may not happen.

> My parents are very conservative and strongly believe what the Bible says and ... they're not wavering from that, but they're also very open ... if I have a question about something or if I'm questioning what the Bible says, they're not going to get angry at me for doing that. They want me to do that.
>
> —Alex

Since we tend to do our devotions on Sundays, we used to ask our kids one at a time what they learned in church that day. Then we'd read and discuss a passage of Scripture (usually a story), share prayer requests, and pray for each other.

Where did we go wrong? We never shared what *we* had learned in church. We were interviewing our kids instead of having a conversation with them. Thanks to our research, now when we ask our kids to share what they learned in church, we talk about what we learned or experienced too. After all, it's a good thing to ask your kids questions about their life and faith. But based on our research, we urge you to make sure you're answering those questions too.

On nights our family has dinner together, we have a tradition of sharing our highs and lows of the day. Because of what we've learned about Sticky Faith, we've added a third question: "How did you see God at work today?"

The first time we added that question to our conversation, our seven-year-old said quickly, "But I can't answer that question."

"Why not?" I asked.

"Because I don't have a job."

Once we explained that we meant "How did you see God *working* today?" she realized she could be part of the discussion.

Often our kids don't have an answer to that question, and that's okay. In fact, as important as the kids' answering that question is that they hear Dave and me answer that question every day.

And don't forget to talk about how God has led you in the past. Many kids don't know when and how their parents started following Christ. Most kids love hearing about when their parents met, when they fell in love, and what their wedding day was like. Why don't we do the same with our faith story? Maybe one of your first Sticky Faith steps is to share with your kids how you became a Christian. What led you down that path? What did it feel like? What surprised you about those early days as a believer? Then talk about what Christ has done in your life. How has he guided you? How has following him changed your behavior? What do you think you would be like if you were not a follower of Christ?

Seek Out Sticky Faith Ideas from Other Parents

Some of our best Sticky Faith ideas come from other wise parents. Margaret is an inspirational mom of eight (yes, eight!) who shared a story with me that shaped her parenting when her children were still young.

In a small town lived two neighbors, Billy and Johnny. Billy's mom was known as one of the best moms in town. She was always baking cookies, sewing outfits for her kids, and volunteering to coordinate school activities.

Johnny's mom, on the other hand, was known as one of the more average moms. She didn't volunteer as much, she didn't bake much, and she didn't know how to sew. All she did was sit and talk with her kids, play games with them, and make simple food.

Everyone in town thought Billy's mom was the best in town.

Except Johnny. Johnny thought *he* had the best mom in town.

After describing that story, Margaret shared with me, "I don't care what other people think of me. I want my kids to think they have a great mom."

For Margaret, greatness has come through vulnerably sharing her life with her kids. In ways that are developmentally appropriate, she shares her feelings and concerns with them. When she faces a major fork in the road and doesn't know which path to take, she shares how much she needs God to guide her steps, and she invites them to pray, just as she is.

When one of her daughters quit cheerleading, the other girls in the squad teased her, bullied her, and even vandalized their home. Depressed, the daughter turned to marijuana as a way to self-medicate. Having failed to notice her daughter's depression and drug use, Margaret later told some of her older children, "I don't know how I missed this in her. I feel like a failure for not realizing what she was going through." Her older kids encouraged her on the spot, pointing out how close they felt to her and helping her see that this was the exception, not the rule, of her mothering.

> So I don't keep anything from my mom ... if I think I'm keeping it from her, I'm not, because she knows it anyway ... but she's a great Christian woman, so I don't feel uncomfortable asking her any questions.
>
> —Aaron

Margaret reports that her college-aged kids now call or visit her regularly to discuss their problems, asking her for advice and for prayer. "I've been really vulnerable so they feel like they can be vulnerable with me. I wouldn't trade that for the world."

A different mom whose kids aren't quite as likely to take such initiative in talking to her has found it helps to ask her kids this simple question: "How can I be praying for you?" Whether it's by text, email, phone, or in person, her kids' answers to that question have helped her learn more about their lives than anything else.

One parent I met takes her kids' prayer requests a step farther. Periodically, she asks both of her sons, one of whom is in college and one of whom is in high school, to write down how they'd like her to pray for them. She makes copies of their prayer requests for her to keep and then she hands back the originals to her sons. When they look at those lists later, they are reminded that their mom is praying for them every day.

One dad told me his goal was to mention God in conversation with his kids every day. Simple. But sticky.

Talk about Your Doubts

Our research suggests that doubt doesn't have to mean the end of faith. In fact, it can inaugurate a whole new richness in your and your kids' relationships with God.

While always keeping in mind what is developmentally appropriate for your kids, you can instill this richer faith into your kids in a number of ways. You can talk about your own doubts and struggles, whether they be more abstract ("I wonder why God lets us choose whether to follow him") or more personal ("I wonder why God allowed your friend to be raised by such an abusive mom and distant dad"). You can also give your kids freedom to share their own questions about particular topics by asking, "What questions do you have, or do you imagine your friends might have?"

You might even turn to the more than one-third of the psalms that are considered laments, either corporately or personally crying out to God in pain, suffering, and doubt. These psalms remind us that it's okay to ask God hard questions. Talking about a verse or two from those psalms will

> *My parents have always been the kind of people who loved for me to learn on my own, to figure out life experiences on my own and to shape my own understanding of who God is.... You know, one thing that I think is the most important in my relationships with my parents is the fact that I see that they have allowed us to learn and they have not made choices for us.*
>
> —Julie

remind your son or daughter that it's okay for them to ask God those hard questions too.

> For more on the psalms of lament,
> see *www.stickyfaith.org.*

Develop Conversation Rituals

"We as parents can't rely on the church. We have to be involved," Kymira declared to me.

Given our Sticky Faith research, Kymira's determination to be involved in her middle school son's life was music to my ears. To put feet to her conviction, she and her husband have developed a weekly discipleship time with their fourteen-year-old son, Kyle. Kymira and her husband take turns every Thursday evening going out for dessert with Kyle and using a youth-ministry small-group curriculum recommended by Kyle's youth pastor as a springboard to talk with Kyle about both Scripture and what's going on in his life. During these weekly parent-son discussions, introverted Kyle has opened up about bullying at school and other peer pressures that he never would have shared during this busy family's typical schedule. According to Kymira, part of the power of this Sticky Faith ritual is that Kyle "has our full and complete attention for an hour ... he has space to have a relationship with us as a teenager instead of as a child."

Maybe this sort of structure won't work with your family, either because of who you are or because of who your child is. Perhaps this sort of curriculum will work for you only for a season. Your goal is to find what works best for your family, which means at times you will need to be creative, organic, and spontaneous, while other times you will need to be organized and systematic.

Whether it's a ritual your family practices together or a ritual that you develop to help your kids have meaningful conversations with other adults, you can build on the following ideas to find something that sticks for your family:

- *Dinner conversation.* When you have dinner together, is it just a time to figure out who needs to be where tomorrow, or do you share about your day? I have already shared questions we ask when we Powells have dinner: "What was your high of the day? What was your low? How did you see God at work?"

  Another question we are considering adding is, "What mistake did you make today?" I know a few other families who discuss this at dinner, and they find that talking about mistakes together carries several benefits. First, it reminds every family member that they are not perfect and need God's grace in the midst of their flaws and sin. Second, it lets kids practice talking about their mistakes with their parents while the stakes are low, which hopefully will make them more likely to talk when the stakes are higher. Finally, it gives family members a chance to apologize to each other for times they have not been kind to each other throughout the day.

- *Creative worship experiences.* During the course of our research, we met one family with middle schoolers who, when their schedule prohibits them from attending their church, have church at home. They encourage their kids to write a new verse to a particular song or hymn they like, or to read a Scripture passage and draw an image that reflects that passage. When they are finished, the family members meet together to share what they learned, drew, or wrote. As this family has found, you don't have to be a musician to involve your kids in creative worship.

- *Special birthdays.* When your child is approaching a birthday that is particularly significant (e.g., becoming a teenager at thirteen or getting a driver's license at sixteen), take them to an overnighter at a hotel. (You can find some great deals online.) Use your meals together as a chance to talk more about what this next year will be like — for your child and for your family.

- *Family goals.* In Colorado, I met Steve, who told me that he and his wife involve his two preteen daughters in setting annual goals — for themselves and for the family — every January. Regularly on Sunday evenings, the family reviews those goals and talks about both progress and changes in direction.

Granted, some of these ideas won't work that well the first time you try them. Some of them will never work in your family. But keep trying. And come up with your own even better ideas.

In an interview with Derek Melleby from the Center for Parent/Youth Understanding, sociologist Tim Clydesdale relays the following about college students, specifically those who have walked away from faith, from his research for the book *The First Year Out.*[5] While he's speaking to youth leaders, his wisdom holds equally true for parents. In many cases, these teens reported having important questions regarding faith during early adolescence (twelve to fourteen years old) that were ignored by their parents or pastors rather than taken seriously and engaged thoughtfully.

"Faith trajectories (along with other life trajectories) are often set in early adolescence. Sadly, most youth ministries are long on fun and fluff and short on listening and thoughtful engagement. The former produces a million paper boats; the latter produces a handful of seaworthy ships. Launching a million paper boats is an amazing spectacle on a clear summer day, but only a ship can weather storms and cross oceans."

Paper boats or seaworthy ships. Which will we build?

sticky reflection and discussion questions

1. What is the best conversation you've had recently with your kid? Why do you think it went so well?

2. How do your kids respond when you try to share with them about your life or faith journey? Why do you think that is? What could you do that would make them even more open to hearing from you?

3. What touchy subject do you need to bring up sometime soon with your kid? What can you do that will make your child less defensive?

4. Which conversation ritual in this chapter, or one that you can think of on your own, would you like to try? When could you give it a whirl with your son or daughter?

a sticky web
of relationships

*Our parents were all close friends and they all did Bible
studies together or just hung out outside of school.
You were always doing something with the church
families and I think that early development of getting
to know the families when I was at a younger age
encouraged the acceptance of us by the time we got
in high school because we had already developed
good relationships with them.*
—Dexter

*All of the high school students and junior high students
sat in the front corner part of the sanctuary. They didn't
really include us a whole lot in the way the service ran.
Every once in a while we were given the chance to lead
worship, but that was once in a blue moon.*
—Megan

On my dad's side of the family, I (Kara) am the oldest of fifteen cousins. When I was growing up, thirty of my relatives
would gather at Grandma and Grandpa Eckmann's house

for holidays. That's far too many people to fit around one table.

So we set up two tables: the adults' table and the kids' table.

We Eckmanns are far from the only family to arrive at this clever and practical two-table solution. I can almost feel you nodding your head as you think about the two tables at your own family gatherings.

At Grandma and Grandpa Eckmann's, the adults ate in the dining room. We kids ate in the TV room.

The adults sat at the fancy dining room table. We sat around card tables.

They ate off nice china. We ate off paper—or if we were lucky, plastic—plates.

They actually had and used napkins—cloth napkins at that. We had our shirtsleeves.

They had pleasant conversation. Somehow our conversation usually degenerated into throwing dinner rolls at each other and holding a Jell-O snorting contest.

> *So, it was kind of ... I don't like this word, but for lack of a better one, segregated, in the sense of the high school students have their thing and then the adults have their thing.*
>
> —Ian

In theory, we were at the same meal. In reality, we had two very different experiences.

That sounds a lot like how adults and kids experience church today. The adults' table is in the bigger, nicer room, and the kids' table is down the hall.

Most churches have adult pastors ... and youth pastors.

Adult worship services ... and student worship services.
Adult mission trips ... and student mission trips.

Do sixteen-year-olds need time to be together and on their own? You bet. As one youth worker told me, "The average sixteen-year-old guy doesn't want to talk about masturbation with Grandma in the room." Neither does Grandma. So that's a nice win-win.

But one of my mantras is that "balance is something we swing through on our way to the other extreme." I'm afraid that's what's happened here. In an effort to offer relevant and developmentally appropriate teaching and fellowship for children and teenagers, we have segregated—and I use that verb intentionally but not lightly—kids from the rest of the church.

And that segregation is causing kids to shelve their faith.

Sticky Findings

We Need to Welcome Children as Jesus Did

I remember the first Bible I received as a child. On the cover was a picture of "Anglo-Saxon Jesus" surrounded by smiling children of all different skin colors. Jesus had this dewy glow, and I think there were fluffy sheep nibbling on tufts of grass in the background. Too cute.

In reality, Jesus' vision for intergenerational relationships was anything but cute. It was and is both radical and revolutionary.

In Luke 9:28–36, Jesus takes Peter, James, and John to a mountain to pray. Jesus' selection of those three disciples and exclusion of the other nine almost certainly fueled feelings of jealousy and insecurity in those left behind. I can almost hear the other nine grumbling under their breath, "What makes Peter so special?"

Soon after, an argument breaks out among all twelve of Jesus' disciples about who is the greatest. Jesus doesn't seem to actually hear the argument, for Luke writes in Luke 9:47 that "knowing their thoughts, [Jesus] took a little child and had him stand beside him." Jesus continues, "Whoever welcomes this little child in my name welcomes me; and whoever welcomes me welcomes the one who sent me. For it is the one who is least among you all who is the greatest" (Luke 9:48).

Thus Jesus places two figures before the disciples: himself, whom they greatly respect, and a child, who in that culture held little intrinsic value. The good news for the disciples is that greatness can be pursued and possessed. The bad news is that this greatness comes from doing something counterintuitive: welcoming a child.

An understanding of the Greek phrasing that Jesus uses in this well-known statement about intergenerational relationships makes his words all the more difficult for the disciples to swallow. The Greek verb Jesus uses here for *welcome* is *dechomai* (pronounced "DECK-oh-my"), which often meant showing hospitality to guests. Thus it carries a certain connotation of servanthood. In the first century, taking care of both guests and children was a task generally fulfilled by members of society who were viewed as different from, and even inferior to, the male disciples—meaning women and slaves.[1]

Thus Jesus was asking the disciples, who had just been arguing about their individual greatness, to show utmost humility by embracing the kids in their midst. According to Jesus, greatness—and dare we say "great" parenting and "great" Christian living—emerges as adults welcome children.

Involvement in All-Church Worship Is Linked with Mature Faith

As we planned our College Transition Project, the FYI research team had hoped to find *one thing* that parents and church leaders could do that would be the silver bullet of Sticky Faith. We had hoped to find one element of kids' church involvement (e.g., Bible study, small groups, mentoring, justice work) that would be significantly related to higher faith maturity—head and shoulders above the rest.

We haven't found that silver bullet. While the study of Scripture, small groups, mentoring, retreats, justice work, and a host of other ministry activities are important, the reality is that kids' spiritual growth is far more complicated than just one silver bullet.

The closest our research has come to that definitive silver bullet is this sticky finding: for high school and college students, there is a relationship between attendance at church-wide worship services and Sticky Faith.

> I wish that there had been an intentional effort by the church to integrate the teenagers in the body with older believers. Although I was able to do this because of my parents' direction, many of the other teenagers were content to remain in youth group, largely separated from the vision and ministry of the church at large. While it may have driven some youth away, I would have liked to see more integration within the larger church body and a clear direction for teenagers to learn what it means to walk with Christ, take up their cross daily, serve others at a cost to oneself, and be disciplined.
>
> —Lilli

Teenagers Who Serve Young Children Build Sticky Faith

Students who serve and build relationships with younger children also tend to have stickier faith. Granted, some teenagers opt to serve in children's ministry because they want to avoid going to "big church." And sure, others volunteer in children's ministry because their school requires service hours.

Yet even with these mixed motives, the high school students we surveyed who served in children's or middle school ministry seemed to have stickier faith in both high school and college. Part of that is likely because of the type of students who volunteer to serve younger kids, but nonetheless, being involved in children's ministry seems to be faith-building.

And while our research didn't specifically examine the effect of teenagers' involvement on the younger children, our guess is that it's not just the teenagers who benefit from that inter-age connection—the younger children do also. When older kids take an interest in younger children, listen to them, and even build a true relationship with them, the young ones glow. (I've seen my own kids' faces light up as twelve-year-olds make an effort to befriend them.) Young children at church tend to assume that adults will pay attention to them, but when "big kids" do, their self-esteem and their love for church skyrocket.

High School Seniors Crave Support from Adults in Their Congregations

As a research team, we weren't all that surprised that of five major sources of support (adults in the congregation, parents, youth workers, friends in youth group, and friends outside of youth group), high school seniors ranked adults in the congregation last.

What did surprise us was how far behind the other four groups they were. One youth group graduate reported that his church "would like to talk about having students involved, but they never really did." Another reflected that church members "wanted nothing to do with us.... I think they see us as kind of scary in that we're the people on the news you know who are dealing drugs and getting pregnant and all those sort of things ... keeping us separate and treating us like we were a hazard." The current chasm between kids and adults in church is greater than we had expected.

By far, the number one way that churches made the teens in our survey feel welcomed and valued was when adults in the congregation showed an interest in them. More than any single program or event, adults' making the effort to get to know the kids was far more likely to make the kids feel like a significant part of their church. One student exclaimed, "We were welcomed not just in youth group; we were welcomed into other parts of the ministry of the church, whether it be in the worship or the praise team on Sunday mornings, or whether it be teaching Sunday school to kids

> I couldn't leave the church each week without being stopped by several adults in the church and engaging in lengthy conversations with each of them. The women of my church were very present when my mother died after my junior year of high school. Basically, I knew at least half of the people in my church fairly well, and they were very supportive of me.
>
> —David

or helping with cleaning and serving … all these other types of things really just brought the youth in and made them feel like they had a place and even feel like they were valued as individuals."

Contact from Adults in the Church Makes a Difference to College Freshmen

Contrary to popular opinion, it's not "out of sight, out of mind" for high school graduates. Contact from at least one adult from the congregation *outside* the youth ministry during the first semester of college is linked with Sticky Faith. Hearing from an adult from their home church—whether via text, email, phone, or something you've perhaps heard of called the US Postal Service—seems to help students take their faith to college with them. In fact, that ongoing contact still makes a difference *three years later.*

College Freshmen Have Difficulty Finding a Church

Once they became college freshmen, we asked the students in our study to share their top difficulties after high school graduation. Here's what they told us:

> Number 1 was friendship.
>
> Number 2 was aloneness.
>
> Number 3 was finding a church.

It's no wonder students have a hard time finding a church. Those who have been sitting at the youth ministry "kids' table" don't know church. They know youth group, not church.

Sticky Faith Made Practical

Chap says a lot of brilliant things, but I think perhaps his most brilliant insight in the last few years is that we need to reverse the ministry adult-to-kid ratio.

What does he mean?

Many children's and youth ministries say they want to have a 1:5 ratio of adults to kids (meaning they want one adult for every five kids) for their Sunday school class or small groups.

What if we reversed that? What if we said we want a 5:1 adult-to-kid ratio—five adults caring for each kid? We're not talking about five Sunday school teachers or five small group leaders. We're also not talking about five adults to whom you outsource the spiritual, emotional, social, and intellectual development of your kids. We're talking about five adults whom you recruit to invest in your kid in little, medium, and big ways. As we at FYI connect with parents across the country, we have seen families experience a 5:1 ratio when they develop a sticky web of relationships for their kids.

Creating a Sticky Web

Extended families often have been the traditional web of caring relationships, and for good reason. Families share holidays and celebrations, attend weddings and funerals, and offer a form of support that lasts generations. Many parents instinctively choose to live close to other family members, and some parents even make career sacrifices in order to stay close to their families. But with the advent of Facebook, Skype, and other new technologies, even distance need not be a barrier to building a sticky web across your extended family.

Parents who are not blessed with grandparents, siblings, and cousins nearby may need to do a bit more work to form a web of relationships, but opportunities abound at church, in the neighborhood, at your child's school, or at your child's activities. Look around you—often the best web is created when you can give as well as receive support for your children. Be one of "the five" for your children's friends, and maybe their parents will be one of the five for yours!

Be Intentional

Sticky social webs don't happen by accident. You need to build those relationships with regular contact. As with most aspects of parenting, we have to be intentional. Just as a spider meticulously creates its web, so we must devote significant time and energy to surrounding our children with intergenerational relationships.

At my church, I've been inspired by one small group of families who have created a sticky web for their kids. While most of the adults in the small group are now grandparents, they started meeting together when their children were newborns. Early on, they decided that they wanted to do more than study the Bible together every week or two; they wanted to be families who stuck together.

Every three months, they bring their calendars to their small group meeting. As is typical in small groups of busy families, they plan several months in advance when they are going to meet. But unlike most small groups, they have taken calendaring to a new level.

This small group has covenanted to make each other's

family events a joint priority. So during their quarterly calendar review, not only do they plan their meetings, but they also share important upcoming family dates and events. All five families mark the Sunday afternoon when Claire has her piano recital. All five families make a note of Mario's Eagle Scout ceremony. All five families jot down the date and time of Isabella's middle school graduation. And as much as possible, the five families try to attend these milestone events.

That's 5:1. That's kingdom community.

Two years ago, Dave and I decided to follow their example by starting an intergenerational group of families to walk through life together. We invited three families to join: one that was in our life stage, one with a newborn, and one couple in their sixties who has mentored us since we were engaged.

We meet together monthly. The first hour or two of our time is devoted to dinner together. The second half of our meeting is focused on whichever book (or more recently, half of a book) we read that month. When possible, we choose books that revolve around topics that our kids can discuss with us for at least a few minutes before they go to another part of our house.

The group would not be the same without the young family just starting to navigate parenthood. Our conversations would not be as deep without the not-so-young-but-still-young-at-heart couple who talks about their love for Jesus and others — both present and past. We could have simply asked three families in our own life stage to meet with us, but we would be the lesser for it.

Maybe that sort of intergenerational small group isn't an option for your family. The good news is that even if you can't develop 5:1 from one cohesive small group, you can create a cluster of relationships that form your own 5:1 constellation.

Maybe you go out of your way to encourage your child's teacher (or small group leader or Sunday school teacher) and invite them over for dinner or dessert with your family.

> *My parents always made sure that I was involved in a lot of adult groups and classes at church and it was there that I felt the most valued and welcome.*
>
> — Bess

Or perhaps your family invites your neighbors to go on a walk or throw a football in your front yard.

Or maybe you schedule regular video calls with adult friends and relatives around the country so your kids feel connected across the miles.

Perhaps you even try to avoid the all-too-common kids' table and adults' table when you have other families or a flock of relatives over for a meal. Maybe you intersperse kids and adults around various tables so cross-generational conversations emerge that never would have otherwise.

In *Big Questions, Worthy Dreams*, Sharon Daloz Parks describes engaging her extended family in intergenerational dialogue at a recent family reunion in which all fifteen relatives intentionally sat around one dinner table: "After we concluded dinner with a yummy cake to celebrate both a fiftieth and a twenty-first birthday, with some trepidation I suggested that around the table we each take a turn sharing something that had been particularly satisfying in the particular year, and something that we expected would be particularly challenging in the year to come. As each one did just that, we were able to catch a glimpse of each other's lives in fresh and shared ways."[2]

With a bit of planning (and perhaps a bit of courage),

most of us can develop a web of adult relationships for our kids that will help develop Sticky Faith.

Be Explicit

There's no need to keep what you're doing a secret from your children. We encourage you to let them in on your 5:1 goal (or 7:1, 10:1, or whatever you're shooting for) and celebrate with you as your family develops its own sticky network. If talking about 5:1 itself feels a bit calculated or forced, you can instead regularly remind your kids of the adults (coaches, teachers, neighbors, church leaders) who care about them and are on your family's team. If you pray at meals or before bed with your child, you could even thank God for the sticky web God is helping to weave.

Recently I met a single mom who had a brilliant idea for helping her son visualize their family's sticky web. In the hallway between their bedrooms, this mom has hung a few large collage picture frames, each of which has several openings for pictures. As her son builds a relationship with an adult — especially with a man — she takes a picture of her son with that adult. Then she places those pictures in the frames to remind them of the amazing adults already surrounding their family. The empty slots in the picture frames reinforce that there are more 5:1 relationships still to come.

Encourage Mentoring

Other adults are often able to speak into your kids' lives in a way that you cannot as their parent. A few years ago I (Kara) heard Tony Dungy, the Super Bowl–winning coach of the Indianapolis Colts, talk about the impact he had seen other adults make on his son.

Tony's high school son was playing football, so every day after school, his son had three hours of football practice. Tony knew the energy that both school and football sucked out of his son, so he urged him to have more than a Pop-Tart for breakfast. The son refused, saying that a Pop-Tart was all he needed. Tony tried to convince his son that he needed more fuel for football, but his son blew off his advice every time.

> I would have liked to see a one-on-one program ... something where every high schooler in the church has an adult in the church that they can look up to and talk to who isn't their parent because there are always barriers with a parent ... someone they can talk to and be honest with.
>
> —Maggie

One morning Tony's son woke up early and stumbled into the kitchen to make himself a large breakfast of bacon and eggs. Tony was tickled that his son had finally heeded his advice. He couldn't resist mentioning to his son, "So I see you're having a bigger breakfast today."

The son replied groggily, "Yeah, my coach said I should."

Here this high school kid was living with one of the most respected NFL coaches in the nation, but since that coach happened to be his dad, he refused to heed his suggestions. It was the coach at the high school who finally got through.

Recognizing the powerful influence of other adults in their kids' Sticky Faith web, many parents include mentoring in their 5:1 plan. Through these empowering relationships, your kids are able to spend time with adults who are farther along in their spiritual journey. Our research has shown that beyond the benefits of the mere presence of mentors, the more adult mentors who seek out the student and help the student apply faith to daily life, the better.[3]

In *The Slow Fade*, Reggie Joiner, Chuck Bomar, and Abbie Smith cast a new vision for the role of a mentor in a young person's life. They write that mentors should ask, "What is God already doing here? — not, What should God be doing here?"[4] In this vision of 5:1 mentoring, adults who meet regularly with your kids will often ask more questions and share more experiences than provide answers.

> For more tangible ideas on mentoring, visit *www.stickyfaith.org*.

Some parents, realizing that the adults they know, trust, and respect are too busy to meet regularly with their teenage children, are seeking less intensive 5:1 connections. One mom I recently met detests gardening, but her teenage daughter loves it. This mom wisely invited one of the women in her church to take her daughter shopping for flower bulbs and then plant them together a few times per year.

You might try taking advantage of structures and programs that already organically pair your kids with other adults by infusing them with 5:1 mentoring vitality. For instance, if your child is already volunteering at your church in some way, talk with the adult who supervises them to see if they'd be open to having a meal with your kid, or your entire family, every once in a while. Try the same with your kid's hockey coach, teacher, or drama coach. Take the time to explain the values and priorities of your family to these influential adults. Sure, these adults are busy, but odds are good that one of the main reasons they do what they do is because they care about kids—including your kids.

Develop a Ritual

In chapter 3, Chap introduced the importance of rituals in students' growing sense of being loved by God. An additional benefit of rituals is that they enable your child to develop 5:1 intergenerational relationships.

For the last few years, Chap and I have enjoyed rubbing shoulders with Reggie Joiner and the great team at reThink Ministries. In *Parenting beyond Your Capacity*, Reggie's coauthor, Carey Nieuwhof, shares a powerful 5:1 intergenerational ritual for his son, Jordan, as he was entering adolescence.

When Jordan turned thirteen, Carey sat down with him and they chose five men whom they both admired. Carey approached the men, asking them to spend one day with Jordan that summer. They could do whatever they wanted to do for that day, but Carey hoped that they would share one spiritual truth and one life truth (i.e., good advice) during the course of their conversations.

A few of the five men took Jordan camping, and another took him to work. One of the five was a police chaplain and took him for a ride in a police cruiser. At the end of the summer, the five men, Jordan, and Carey gathered for a barbeque, and Jordan shared from a journal what had impacted him the most during each of those five special days. Jordan presented each of the five with a Bible with their name inscribed on the cover. Each of the five then took a few minutes to comment on their time with Jordan and ways they saw God at work in Jordan's life. Afterward, they all gathered around Jordan and laid hands on him in prayer. Many of the men shared, "I wish someone had done that for me when I was thirteen."[5]

When Carey's second son, Sam, completed the same mentoring process when he was turning thirteen, one of the highlights was the five mentors sharing how their time with Sam had impacted them. In fact, that final barbeque dinner was so powerful that the five men asked if they could get together every year, if that was okay with Sam. Sam said it was, and they are already planning for next year's dinner.

Develop Diverse Friendships

You have enormous control over which adults walk into your house and into your family's life, so consider intentionally building friendships with adults of all ages. One student we interviewed reported about a couple who was close with her parents: "I guess I consider them family friends, but I wouldn't mind hanging out with them, just me and them. Like I would go to coffee with her if I had the chance.... It's just ... very natural, like another set of parents almost."

> There was a friend of my dad who actually gave me a One Year Bible, just because he cared about what I was going through at the time.
>
> —Adrea

Ask Your Kids Who They Want to Spend Time With

One friend of mine has asked her daughters to name five adults they respect and want to be like. Now my friend knows just who to invite over for dinner on a free evening.

Send Your Kids to Work with Friends

One family we know has a special ritual that involves sending their two sons to work with men they respect. They asked each man to let their sixteen-year-old sons shadow them for two hours. At some point during those two hours, their sons were given a few minutes to ask each man questions, such as "What's the hardest part of being a man? What's the hardest part of following God? Looking back over your life, what do you wish you had done differently?" Their sons still stay in touch with these men, and they also seem to assume that they can and should continue to seek out other male mentors now that they are in college.

Ask for Experiences, Not Gifts

For her kids' birthdays, one mom I met during our research asked friends or relatives who might normally give a gift to her children to give them experiences instead. Instead of giving her kids a gift certificate or a new sweater, these folks take them to a movie or out to dinner, thereby building a stickier relationship.

Exchange Prayer Requests

Ask your kids to share prayer requests with other adults, and vice versa. Encourage both to touch base periodically to see how God moves.

Ask for Special Advice or Encouragement

Invite adults who are close to your child to gather together, perhaps at a birthday or holiday celebration, and share words of advice or encouragement with your child. If they write these down and present them in a book or folder, then your child will have a permanent reminder of their 5:1 support team.

One family decided to host their son's baptism at their home instead of at their church facility. They invited family members as well as church members who had invested in their son to come and bring their eighth grader a simple gift with spiritual symbolism that they could explain to their son, such as a small painting or sculpture or something from nature. These parents experienced the power of the Jewish *bar mitzvah* in their own home with their family and close friends.

Graduation is a natural time for asking for advice and encouragement. Have kids invite adults who have been special to them to their high school graduation parties. Provide a journal in which guests can write down their words of advice and encouragement. And better yet, have your kids tell each guest (either in person or on the invitation) how he or she has impacted them. Not only will the adults feel thanked but also the kids will begin to understand and appreciate how much other people have contributed to their lives—and realize the importance of doing that themselves someday.

Creating a Sticky Web at Your Church

Those of us who are involved in a church have a natural springboard for our 5:1 relationships. My church, Lake Avenue Church, is moving toward more intergenerational worship and relationships. And yet last year, my seven-year-old daughter showed me how far we still have to go.

It was our Good Friday evening service and our family

arrived a few minutes early. As we were waiting for the service to start, Krista pointed at the front of the worship center and asked, "Mommy, what are those yellow tubes? There are so many of them."

I smiled and answered, "Krista, those are the pipes for the organ."

"Mommy, what's an organ?"

My amusement at my daughter's first question quickly changed to dismay. No one, including me or my husband, had ever explained to her all of the dynamics and elements of our worship service. How could she feel a part of the broader community if she felt like a confused outsider? So I made it my mission at that Good Friday service to explain everything. I whispered in her ear, "Hear that music? That's coming from the organ."

"See that woman? She's making announcements."

"Can you read those words on the screen? They're reminding us what Jesus did by dying for us on the cross."

Here I am a champion for intergenerational ministry and my own daughter didn't understand what was happening in intergenerational worship. It was a good reminder that we grown-ups take a lot for granted, and children have a lot to learn. So here we will look at some concrete ways we can make sure that our children have contact with adults and are fully integrated into the life of the church.

Integrate 5:1 Thinking into Existing Church Activities

As with your own family, 5:1 won't happen at your church by accident. Your church will need to be intentional in its planning and programming.

The good news is that as your church moves its programs toward 5:1, it doesn't have to start from scratch. Your children's ministry, your youth ministry, and your church are already hosting events that with a bit of planning and some broader invitations could easily become more intergenerational.

Perhaps if your adult Sunday school class is going to serve food to those who are homeless, you could suggest inviting the middle school kids to join you.

Or if you're a mom, you can encourage your daughter's friends and their moms to join you and your daughter at the upcoming Saturday Women's Tea.

If you're a dad, you could invite your son's friends and their dads to join you and your son at the men's annual steak fry (whatever that is; does it literally mean men fry steaks? I've never been to one).

The bottom line is that if your church plans ahead, you can capitalize on momentum from existing events instead of starting from scratch. As you look at your church calendar, consider ways to be a voice — loud or subtle — for change toward more intergenerational connections for your kids and others.

Include Youth in Corporate Worship

A youth ministry I heard about recently is taking larger leaps toward sticky intergenerational relationships through their worship. Like many youth ministries, this ministry met twice per week — once on Sundays and once on Wednesdays. The youth pastor, along with some kids, parents, and other church leaders, started asking, "Why are we meeting twice per week? What's the purpose of each meeting?"

They realized they were more or less offering the same sort of worship, teaching, and fellowship twice every week. They also realized that hardly any of their students were involved in the larger church.

So they canceled Sunday youth group. No more Sunday meetings. Instead, kids are now fully integrated into the church on Sundays. Kids are greeters, they serve alongside adults on the worship music team, they are involved in giving testimonies, and they even give chunks of the sermon from time to time. The youth pastor described the power of this 5:1 shift: "We knew that this would change our kids. What has surprised us is how much it has changed our church."

Another church decided to make their youth choir the main choir for the primary 11:00 a.m. Sunday service. They knew they risked that the service might shrink in size until the only attendees left were the teenagers and their parents. But the opposite ended up happening. That 11:00 a.m. service became one of the most popular services as adults who had invested in those kids as Sunday school teachers and confirmation sponsors, along with other adults who simply cared about kids, couldn't wait to have the teenagers lead them in worship music.

I'm not saying that every church should cancel their Sunday youth group or disband their adult choir. But I am saying that the parents in churches should be asking, "How can we increase adult-kid interaction during worship?"

As we've interacted with churches nationwide, we've noticed that smaller churches are often less likely to have "full service" children's and youth ministry programs and thus tend to already have more opportunities for intergenerational relationships. That's to be affirmed, but every church —regardless of size—can still look to either increase their opportunities for adult-kid interaction or increase the strategic impact of the opportunities they already offer.

One church decided to display a onetime powerful and sticky image of how kids can and should be involved through worship. One Sunday during worship music, the regular worship team comprised solely of adults began singing and playing their instruments, just like normal.

Suddenly a teenager came forward from the audience and tapped the shoulder of the guitarist standing at the center of the stage. The kid held out both his hands, and the adult musician handed his guitar to the kid and walked off the platform. The kid started playing the guitar.

A few moments later, another kid came from the side of the platform and tapped the adult drummer on the shoulder. The same thing happened: the adult drummer stood up, handed his drumsticks to the kid, and walked off the stage. The kid resumed the drumming.

Within a few minutes, kids had stepped up to the platform and taken the places of the bass player, keyboardist, and lead singer. What had been a 100 percent adult worship team became a 100 percent student worship team. Regardless of their age, all members of the congregation were swept up in a new spirit of enthusiastic worship.

Then the senior pastor got up to preach. After a few minutes, a voice from backstage yelled, "If you're serious about involving us, we have to go all the way." From backstage, a teenager appeared, walked up to the senior pastor, and tapped the senior pastor's shoulder. The senior pastor stopped preaching, handed the microphone to the kid, and walked off the platform. The kid finished the sermon.

There's something very powerful and beautiful about that sticky imagery. We're so used to kids being segregated off in the youth room or in their Sunday school class that when we get glimpses of kids being involved in the full church, we know it's right. We know it contributes to Sticky Faith.

As much as I love that imagery, if I could wave my Sticky Faith wand (still looking for how to invent one of those, by the way), there's one thing I would change: I wish the adults and kids had actually led worship and preached together. After all, our research doesn't suggest that kids need to *replace* adults in leading worship. Our vision is that kids and adults experience worship *together*.

Find Compromise If Your Kid Doesn't Want to Go to Church

About half of the time I share the importance of intergenerational worship with parents, I get asked, "Should I make my kid go to church?" Believe me, as much as I am an advocate for intergenerational worship, I'm not naïve about how teenagers feel about sitting through church. I felt that way a fair amount myself as a kid.

This is a tough question, one I wish we could discuss over coffee so I could ask more questions about your kids and family. But not knowing your specific family, let me say this: while your long-term goal is intergenerational connection primarily in and with a church family, the first hurdle is to help your kid to feel like they are part of something they are choosing and enjoy. Forced friendships do not work very well for adolescents. Depending on the issues your child is dealing with and why they do not want to go, perhaps you could consider the following:

1. Make sure your kids know that, as important as church is to you as the parent, you respect their desire not to

go. At the same time, let them know that being a part of God's family is an important part of your family's life.

2. Find ways to connect your child to Christian friends in casual or organic settings. As these intentional relationships develop and deepen, your child will have a greater internal incentive to get involved.

3. Find out what, if any, faith activities they would like or are willing to be part of. (I would do all you can to steer away from "making" them attend.) Perhaps a parachurch group, or a different church's worship service, or a Bible study would help them feel more connected and involved. Sometimes a friend's church or youth group will become a place where they can connect with a faith community.

4. In the end, do your best to seek a compromise. Depending on their age and your family's circumstance, ask your child to attend with you once a month, especially if they are plugged in somewhere else, and to do it out of love and respect for you and your faith. If they are attending a different church, you should probably offer to attend that church with them monthly also.

Develop Rituals for Your Church

In addition to your family, your church might provide opportunities for 5:1 rituals. San Clemente Presbyterian Church is a congregation fifty miles south of Fuller's Pasadena campus that had already embraced the importance of intergenerational relationships before FYI even started our College Transition Project. As a result, while other churches are taking 5:1 baby steps, San Clemente Presbyterian is sprinting ahead. Much of their intergenerational DNA centers on grade-based rituals, or "rites of passage," that you might want to suggest that your own church consider.

> Families of first graders gather with their children every year for a first communion.

> In both second and sixth grade, children receive a Bible from the church inscribed with a note from their parents.

> Fifth graders and their families come together to celebrate a traditional Passover dinner.

> When students reach junior high, they are taken on a confirmation retreat and officially become members of the San Clemente body.

> At the beginning of their senior year of high school, students hike to the top of Half Dome in Yosemite with the youth pastor, the youth ministry volunteers, and the senior pastor. According to Dr. Tod Bolsinger, the senior pastor, "This tradition is so important I have parents of elementary age children telling me to keep in shape so I can take their child on this rite-of-passage hiking experience."[6]

> At the end of the school year, the church hosts a blessing ceremony for all high school students, graduating seniors, parents, and congregation members.

> For more practical intergenerational ideas for your church, visit *www.stickyfaith.org.*

Every year at this church, students experience 5:1 rituals that break down barriers between the adults' table and the kids' table.

The small groups at my church have also really been a big presence in staying connected with us ... they've been coming up with projects and ... ways that they can stay connected with the college students and so that's really nice too, especially when my roommates find out about it because they're not particularly strong Christians.... During Halloween they sent care packages and it was just kind of neat because my roommates see this huge box on the porch and it's full of candy and snacks and stuff and they're like, "Who sent this?!" So it's nice to be able to share with them who it was.

—Bethany

Add Intergenerational Activities to Your Church Calendar

As we have networked with and learned from other churches moving toward 5:1, we've been encouraged by their creativity. Here are a handful of innovative ideas that you might want to experiment with or, better yet, use as a springboard to come up with even more creative ideas.

> *Hold a technology tutorial.* Gather your kids with senior adults and let the teenagers teach the seniors how to send text messages so they can keep in touch with their grandkids.
>
> *Throw a junior-senior dance.* Invite high school kids and senior adults together for a dance (or depending on your denomination, maybe a banquet). Play fifties music and let the boogying begin.
>
> *Schedule a new Christian birthday party.* Once a year, schedule a big birthday party for folks of all ages who've become Christians. Decorate with streamers

and balloons, serve cake and ice cream, and invite your entire church to celebrate the "new creations" of all ages.

Have teens worship with the children. Once a quarter, invite teenagers to join the children's worship experience. Involve both little kids and big kids in the worship music, the announcements, and the teaching.

Go camping. Get away for a weekend with other church families and experience the beauty of God's creation together under the stars. Share stories around the campfire as you roast marshmallows.

A Few Final Notes

In our list of 5:1 ideas above, you might have noticed that many of them revolve around uniting kids and senior adults. Both groups often feel marginalized and underappreciated. Plus there's a special tenderness teenagers hold for senior adults, and vice versa. (Remember the tight bond between seventy-eight-year-old Mr. Fredrickson and young Russell in the movie *Up*?)

As theologian Stanley Hauerwas reminds us, providing ways for senior adults to build meaningful relationships with teenagers allows those seniors to reach their full kingdom potential. Hauerwas convincingly argues that when people age, "they cannot

> There's one or two elderly ladies that send me cards at college sometimes or those are the ones that I do talk to the most when I do go back to my old church and say "hi" to everybody. Mostly it's just small talk and little stuff that we talk about, but it's still good to have that little grandma figure with you.
>
> —Rajeev

move to Florida and leave the church to survive on its own. For Christians, there is no 'Florida'—even if they happen to live in Florida. That is, we must continue to be present to those who have made us what we are so that we can make future generations what they are called to be. Aging among Christians is not and cannot be a lost opportunity."[7] So helping your kids connect with senior adults—whether in your church, family, or neighborhood—is a great way to get your 5:1 train moving down the tracks.

> For more Sticky Faith ideas involving grandparents, visit *www.stickyfaith.org.*

Last but not least, the families we know who are best at using 5:1 to move away from the adults' and kids' tables dichotomy often use service or justice work as a springboard for intergenerational relationships. When you're painting a wall or feeding someone who's homeless, most of the barriers and awkwardness of age differences quickly fall away. Our next chapter is devoted exclusively to Sticky Justice, so as you turn the page, please continue reading with your 5:1 glasses on.

sticky reflection and discussion questions

1. To what degree are your kids at the "kids' table" in your life and at your church? What is good about that? What might be problematic?

2. What are the advantages of trying to surround each of your kids with five adults who care about them? What are the costs?

3. In your role in your church, how (if at all) can you help change your church's culture? While you may have a limited sphere of influence at your church, what changes can you suggest in your own sphere?

4. What ideas do you have to help your kids connect with other adults and move toward the 5:1 ratio?

5. How would you explain your 5:1 goal to your kids?

sticky justice

My parents are both very serving people,
both in the church and outside of the church.
When I see that example, I see the kind
of Christlike service that they hold.
—Missy

My parents have always been involved in some
ministry at church and they've always had
a revolving door at our house to let people
come and go. Their lives themselves have been
a good witness to me growing up.
—Albert

If I asked your kids, what would they say is at the heart of what it means to be part of your family?

In other words, how would your kids finish this sentence: "Our family is ..."?

My (Kara's) husband grew up with a very strong sense of what it meant to be a Powell. Both by their example and by their words, Dave's parents instilled in him that being part of the Powell family meant you were hardworking and looked for ways to humbly serve others.

Dave and I are trying to instill a similar sense of family identity into our own kids. We even use the language of "In our family, we ..." or "In our family, we don't ..."

We've also tried to define this family identity through our prayers. When our firstborn was still in the womb, we settled on four phrases that summarize our deepest desires for who our family is and will become. We pray these four phrases over our kids every night, and they are part of how we pray for our kids as a couple too. In fact, they capture who Dave and I want to be.

We pray that the Lord will make us:

> leaders and learners.
>
> people of gentle strength.
>
> content risk-takers.
>
> folks who love and serve God and others.

This last phrase is the uber-prayer. It's the linchpin from which the other three flow. If we had to pick just one phrase to pray, it would be that we Powells are folks who love and serve God and others.

In many ways, that's what this entire book is about: how can we be parents who love and serve God and others, and who raise kids who do likewise? But in this chapter we're going to focus on one slice of that phrase: how do we raise kids who serve? In other words, how can we plant a vision for kingdom service so deeply in our kids that they can't help but offer love and hope to those in need?

Last month I met a family that shares this longing that their kids have a heart for service. They have made a commitment as a family to help folks who are homeless not by giving them money but by buying them a bag of groceries instead. As their three daughters were growing up, the parents consistently explained, "Our family does not give money when we are approached on the street. We buy food instead." When approached by someone who was homeless, the parents would run into a nearby supermarket and buy a bag of groceries for the person in need, often with their daughters in tow.

Recently their seventeen-year-old daughter, Kristen, was heading alone into a grocery store when she was approached by a homeless man who asked her for money. Even though Kristen was alone, she repeated the family mantra to him: "Our family does not give money. We buy food instead." She walked into the grocery store and spent $17 of her own to buy him groceries.

As Kristen retold the story to her mom, her mom waited with bated breath, wondering if Kristen would ask her to reimburse her the $17.

Kristen didn't.

In that moment, Kristen showed Sticky Faith.

I love this story and applaud this family. I hope that my kids someday use their own money to buy groceries for someone who is in need. I believe Jesus wants us to meet the immediate needs of others.

These days I'm meeting more families who realize that giving someone $17 worth of groceries is an important first step on the long path of long-term change. That vital first step needs to be followed by other steps, like talking with the homeless man to find out why he is homeless. Or understanding social-service and job-training resources in our city well enough that we can work with him to identify ways he could get his own food for weeks and months to come. It's that sort of systemic approach to helping others that enables us and our kids (not to mention the homeless man) to turn the corner from short-term service to sustainable justice.

Service is giving someone who is thirsty a glass of cold water. It's a noble act. And let's be honest, sometimes that's all we have the time or ability to do.

But justice goes deeper. Justice asks why the person couldn't get their own glass of water, helps them figure out how to get their own glass of water, and works with them so they can help others get their own water too.

Is it harder? You bet.

Does it take longer? Unfortunately, yes.

But does it lead to deeper transformation? Absolutely.

As we dive into our Sticky Findings on how pursuing justice can make faith real for our kids, let's begin by defining and describing biblical justice.

Sticky Findings

Justice Is a Biblical Value and Theme

Last month a leader told me that his church "freaks out" when he uses the word *justice*. *Justice* seems to trigger one of two images in his church members' minds: radical druggie hippies from the 1960s or "liberal" believers who talk more about freedom and rights than Jesus or salvation.

I responded, "Then your church hasn't read the Bible. The Bible talks about justice as one of God's core attributes, and it's a word that we have to reclaim."

Just a smattering of Scripture passages reveals God's deep concern for justice:

"Follow justice and justice alone, so that you may live and possess the land the LORD your God is giving you" (Deut. 16:20).

"Cursed is anyone who withholds justice from the foreigner, the fatherless or the widow" (Deut. 27:19a).

"Arise, LORD, in your anger; rise up against the rage of my enemies. Awake, my God; decree justice" (Ps. 7:6).

"The LORD works righteousness and justice for all the oppressed" (Ps. 103:6).

"Blessed are those who act justly, who always do what is right" (Ps. 106:3).

"I will make justice the measuring line and righteousness the plumb line" (Isa. 28:17a).

"For I, the LORD, love justice" (Isa. 61:8a).

"But let those who boast boast about this: that they understand and know me, that I am the LORD, who exercises kindness, justice and righteousness on earth, for in these I delight" (Jer. 9:24 TNIV).

"But let justice roll on like a river, righteousness like a never-failing stream!" (Amos 5:24).

"He has shown all you people what is good. And what does the LORD require of you? To act justly and to love mercy and to walk humbly with your God" (Mic. 6:8 TNIV).

"And will not God bring about justice for his chosen ones, who cry out to him day and night? Will he keep putting them off?" (Luke 18:7).

"God presented Christ as a sacrifice of atonement, through the shedding of his blood—to be received by faith. He did this to demonstrate his justice" (Rom. 3:25a TNIV).

Biblical Justice Meets All Sorts of Needs

Another word in Scripture closely linked with the term *justice* is *shalom*. We tend to think of shalom as "peace," as in an individual's subjective sense of peace (e.g., "I feel peace about meeting my upcoming deadline") or as in the absence of violence and physical conflict (e.g., "We are praying for peace in the Middle East").

Those are both accurate, but like our understanding of justice, our understanding of shalom is too small. In describing shalom and its relationship to justice, Dr. Nicholas Wolterstorff, professor of philosophical theology at Yale University, writes, "The state of shalom is the state of flourishing in all dimensions of one's existence: in one's relation to God, in one's relation to one's fellow human beings, in one's relation to nature, and in one's relation to oneself. Evidently justice has something to do with the fact that God's love for each and every one of God's human creatures takes the form of God desiring the shalom of each and every one."[1]

Far more than just a warm and fuzzy feeling, God's shalom means we right wrongs around us — both locally and globally — so that all can experience the holistic flourishing that God intends. There is no shortage of opportunities to right wrongs — for those in poverty, those who are handicapped, those who are imprisoned, those who are marginalized, or those who are entering a new country or culture. You and your family can offer shalom by personally interacting with these folks or by working to improve our political, economic, and educational systems.

Kids Want to Be Involved in Service and Justice Work

Here's some good news: the students we surveyed have told us they want to extend God's shalom to the least, the last, and the lost. We asked graduating high school seniors what they wished they had had more of in youth group. Of the thirteen options we provided, their number one answer was "time for deep conversation."

Second was mission trips.

Third was service projects.

Last was games. (Granted, a survey of seventh-grade boys may have yielded a different hierarchy.)

Even MTV is realizing that justice is "in" with kids and young adults. While MTV continues to air shows that elevate decadence like *My Super Sweet 16* and *MTV Cribs*, MTV is also planning to broadcast reality TV shows that showcase kids traveling across the country, making wishes come true for deserving locals who face debilitating diseases or are trapped in poverty.[2] Wouldn't it be great if someday MTV devoted an entire show to kids of faith engaged in Sticky Justice?

Short-Term Mission Work Does Not Lead to Lasting Transformation

Service and justice work—as we currently do them—are not sticking like we'd hope. More than two million US teens go on mission trips annually.[3] While that's something to applaud, for five out of six of them, the trips don't have much impact on their lives.[4]

Various research projects conducted by two friends and

colleagues from other schools, such as Robert Priest from Trinity Evangelical Divinity School and Kurt Ver Beek from Calvin College, suggest that our current service experiences might not be producing the spiritual and relational bang we would hope for—at least not in the long term. For example:

> The explosive growth in the number of short-term mission trips among both kids and adults has not translated into similarly explosive growth in the number of career missionaries.
>
> It's not clear whether participation in service trips causes participants to give more money to alleviate poverty once they return to life as usual.
>
> Service trips do not seem to reduce participants' tendencies toward materialism.[5]

To paraphrase the *Field of Dreams* mantra, if we send them, they will grow.

Maybe.

Service Is Stickier When It Hits Close to Home

A few years ago, MTV conducted a nationwide survey in order to understand how and why youth in America are active in social causes.[6] The top five reasons kids are not involved are:

1. It's just not for me (18 percent).
2. I like to hang out with friends (15 percent).
3. I don't have enough time (14 percent).
4. I don't know how to get started (14 percent).
5. I want to see concrete results (8 percent).

Sixty-two percent say the issues that matter most to them are those that have touched them or someone they know.

Seventy percent of kids involved in activism report that their parents' encouragement played a major factor in their choice to get involved.

The top two factors that would motivate kids to be more involved are:

1. If they could do the activity with their friends.
2. If they had more time to volunteer or more convenient volunteer activities.[7]

As we think about our role in creating space for our kids to experience sticky service, one theme emerges from the MTV findings: justice will be stickier when it hits kids close to home. It needs to be in their home *literally*, as we as parents exemplify, encourage, and actually participate with our kids in righting wrongs around them. It needs to hit close to home *thematically*, as we help our kids understand how particular injustices relate to their lives. It needs to hit home *personally*, as we expose our kids to actual people who have been oppressed, thereby giving injustice a face and a name. And justice ministry needs to hit home *relationally*, as we help our kids serve others in partnership with their friends.

Sticky Faith Made Practical

Find Sticky Causes
That Matter to Your Kid

The parents I've met who are best at engaging their kids in Sticky Justice are those who connect their kids with sticky causes—causes that hit kids close to home.

Recently I heard about one family that has found a sticky cause through their church, Frontline Community Church in Grand Rapids, Michigan. In October 2009, a team from the church did a short-term mission trip in Port-au-Prince, Haiti. In Port-au-Prince, the team met Kelencia, a two-year-old who wore size-one diapers.

The church team was told that Kelencia had a hole in her heart, and Haitian doctors reported that if she didn't have surgery, there was a very good chance she would die within the year. The team called hospitals all over Michigan, and a hospital in Ann Arbor agreed to do the $100,000 surgery for free. All the church had to do was raise a few thousand dollars for a round-trip plane ticket and other expenses like visas, clothes, and food for Kelencia while she was in the US.

The church's teenagers volunteered to raise the funds. Working in small groups, the kids poured every ounce of their God-given creativity into their fundraising. One group of high school girls learned how to knit, and they spent two straight weekends knitting washcloths and dish towels, which they then sold, raising $200.

Another small group of kids bought a bunch of jelly beans and created a poem based on the different-colored jelly beans and how they related to Scripture. They packaged them in small baggies with the poem and Kelencia's story attached and sold them to friends, family, and complete strangers. They made $250.

One tenth grader, Ian, worked with his small group to collect soda cans. But Ian's interest in Haiti didn't end at can collecting. Ian wanted to meet Kelencia and see Haiti firsthand, so he submitted an application to go with the churchwide mission team back to Port-au-Prince. When Ian's application was accepted, Ian's dad, Pat, realized that if he also went on the trip, he and his son would have a common touch point that would last for life.

So Pat asked his son if it would be all right for him to go on the trip too. Ian's reply will sound familiar to parents of teenagers: "All right, as long as you don't crowd me."

Pat wisely replied, "I'll do my best and if I get out of line, just correct me, and I'm sure we'll get along fine."

Ian and the other students ended up raising $2,200 for Kelencia's expenses, which was more than she needed. The entire church celebrated the exciting news that four months later, Ian and Pat and others from the church would visit with Kelencia in Haiti. Three months after that, Kelencia would fly to Michigan for her lifesaving surgery.

Three days after the church celebration, the major January 12, 2010, earthquake hit Haiti. The church didn't know for twenty-four hours whether Kelencia had made it. Finally the church received a phone call and news that Kelencia's entire town was leveled, and she didn't survive.

The church's Now Generation pastor, Matthew Deprez, describes what that experience was like for the teenagers. "That night we made an announcement to the kids who had just raised all this money for her. Words can't describe what that night was like. Students wept for hours. It was horrible."

Ian's response was a little different. He went to Matthew and asked, "Are you 100 percent sure that Kelencia is dead?"

Matthew's honest answer was, "No, but we are 99 percent sure."

Ian replied, "I won't believe it until it's 100 percent. I am hanging on to that 1 percent."

Ian's optimism was well founded. Twenty-four hours later, the church received another phone call from Haiti saying that Kelencia was alive, and she barely had a scratch on her.

In four months, Ian and his dad were at the orphanage with members of their church and met Kelencia face-to-face. Ian's time with Kelencia and the other needy children at the orphanage strengthened his interest in studying to be a teacher.

During the trip, the team closed out each day by answering a simple question: "What was your 'moment' of the day?" Usually Ian answered before Pat, and Ian talked about who he met, or orphans he played with, or what he had learned about Haiti. Pat recalled after the trip, "When it was my turn to describe my 'moment,' my honest answer would have been that the highlight of my day was seeing my son describe *his* highlight. I knew that would embarrass Ian, so I never gave that as an answer. But that was the 'moment' of each day for me."

You might not be able to go to Haiti. But I'm guessing that every day, you and your son or daughter hear news that reminds you of what's wrong with our world.

For example, I was stunned last year when an article in the *New York Times* profiled segregated proms.[8] I had no idea such proms still existed, but at a few public schools in Georgia and Tennessee that offer only one official prom, parents have banded together to offer an unofficial "white" prom and "black" prom. (By the way, did you catch that it's the *parents* who are behind these segregated proms?)

I'm not sure if I am more mad or sad. But I do know this: if I were a parent in these areas, I'd be talking about this close-to-home injustice with my kids, brainstorming ways we could right this wrong.

If your child has had a bumpy academic road during middle school or high school, they might be burdened to tutor or mentor elementary school kids.

If you have teenage daughters, you might find that they have a special connection with victims of sex trafficking.

What is it that strikes close to home for your children? If you don't have an answer to that question, get one by asking your kids.

Serve Together as a Family

Perhaps your kids are serving through your church's youth ministry and you are volunteering in a different ministry. While that's good, you might be missing out on the great impact of serving together.

Based on her extensive study of thirty-two congregations from diverse denominations and geographical regions in the United States, Diana Garland has seen the impact of family members serving together instead of separately. She has found that "unlike family service, individual projects can actually be a strain on family life, pulling family members away from one another rather than together in shared activity."[9] Family projects and service opportunities, even if just for a few hours, give families common experiences and common memories. Families can serve together any number of ways, from packing lunches for the homeless to going on mission trips together.

Rob is a parent of three young children whose own commitment to serving the poor was launched by his parents' passion for missions. Rob remembers, "My parents always had a focus on missions; growing up, my dad went on a lot of trips on his own to serve in different places. When I was in middle school, my dad came back from one of those trips and said he wasn't going to go again until we could all go as a family."

When Rob was a ninth grader, his whole family spent ten weeks serving at a missionary-run farm school for two hundred boys in Honduras. The family worked on the farm for half the day and attended classes the other half.

Rob's dad had been to this location before, so he was able to share ahead of time what to expect and the intent of the trip. While they were on-site, Rob's parents reminded them, especially in the midst of hard work or Rob's missing his friends and activities at home, "This is why we are here. This is what God has called us to do." This trip deeply impacted Rob's faith and that of his brothers, two of whom had been adopted by the family from another Latin American country.

Now Rob is thinking about how to replicate those kinds of experiences with his own kids. He notes, "That's definitely an outflow of the priorities of the home I grew up in. Those seeds were planted a long time ago."

That's justice that sticks.

Make Justice Work
not an Event but a Process

Our research indicates the good news that kids want to serve. But as we've seen, the bad news is that we're falling far short of the fruit we could be yielding from the justice vine. Justice work is more likely to stick when it's not an event but a process.

Over the past few years, we at FYI, in collaboration with Dave Livermore of the Global Learning Center at Grand Rapids Theological Seminary and Terry Linhart of Bethel College (Indiana), have convened two summits of short-term missions experts for honest discussions about what research says we are — and are not — accomplishing through our mission work.[10] One theme repeatedly emerges: we need to do a better job walking with our kids before, during, and after their mission experience.[11]

The Before/During/After Model

As a result of our summits and our surveys of kids, we at FYI recommend an experiential education framework originally proposed by Laura Joplin[12] and later modified and tested by Dr. Terry Linhart[13] on youth mission trips, called the Before/During/After Model.[14]

The Before/During/After Model

Step 1. Before: Framing

A sticky service or justice experience starts when we help our kids frame the sometimes mind-blowing and other times menial experiences that await them. If your kids are going to be interacting with folks who are homeless, ask them to imagine what it's like to live on the streets. If your son is interested in a short-term mission trip, sit down with him, find out why he's interested, and help him think about how the trip might open his eyes. No matter the experience, think ahead with your kids about the people with whom they'll be interacting and what they can learn about themselves, others, and God during their justice work.

> For more on the Before/During/After model, as well as Sticky Justice, visit *www.stickyfaith.org.*

Step 2. During: Experience and Reflection

The main component in students' learning during their actual service is the cycle of experience and reflection. The barrage of experiences on a typical service adventure comes so fast and furious that our kids often feel as if they're sprinting through a museum, barely viewing its masterpieces out of the corners of their eyes. Even if we as parents aren't with our kids during their service work, we hope their adult chaperones are committed to giving our kids space to catch their breath and ask questions to decipher the sticky meaning behind their observations, thoughts, and feelings.

Some questions that might help your kids process their experience include:

- What was your favorite part?
- What was the hardest part?
- What did you do well?
- What mistakes did you make?
- How did you see God at work?
- How did you see others being used by God?
- What questions did you have that you've gotten at least partial answers to?
- What new questions does your experience raise for you?

Step 3. After: Initial Debriefing

The goal of the third step is to talk with our sons and daughters soon after they return home to help them identify what changes they hope will stick long term. If you have the chance, sit down with your child and ask questions like:

- How did God work through you? What does that say about how God might want to work through you now that you're home?

- How has your experience shaped your view of service and justice? What difference might that make now?

- What have you learned about people who are poor or who are different from you? How do you want that to shape you now?

- What ideas do you have to help this be more than just a onetime experience and instead be something that impacts your life?

Step 4. After: Ongoing Transformation

In the fourth step, we as parents over the next several weeks help our kids with ongoing transformation, like connecting the dots between having lunch with a homeless man in Baltimore and having lunch with a new kid in their school cafeteria the following month.

In her survey of more than fifty churches from various denominations and regions in the United States, Diana Garland found that families who serve "want somehow to ground what they are doing in their lives of faith. They want their service to make sense as Christians."[15] This before/during/after approach to service can help your entire family move your service and justice work from the shallow end of mere activity to the deep end of discussion and growth.

One parent who's also a pastor shared the importance of talking with his four kids before and after their justice work. He said, "Both before and after our kids go to serve someplace, we look for opportunities to process with our kids in conversation. We need to be very intentional and attentive for opportunities, but not force anything. It is counterproductive when my kids 'smell' us trying too hard.

"My wife, Suzanne, puts it this way: 'We carefully listen and look for doors that might be open. We push very gently and if they open, we walk in.' For each child, the doors and the times to knock are different. For one, a direct question will shut the door hard, while another is delighted to be invited out for a soda and a long discussion. One child needs gentle prodding and lots of time and space; another needs only some focused attention and a single question. For one, the discussions happen along the way; for another, they are the main event. For one, they happen on a slow weekend afternoon; for another they are strictly a late-night affair."

He continued, "We believe these conversations are huge in their lives. God gives us the privilege, if we will, of walking with our kids as they process God's leading and transformation. These discussions don't just magically happen. We can't quantify or compartmentalize what is accomplished as we listen, as we ask open-ended questions, as we discover together, and as we pray. But if we abandon the effort to participate in these discussions, we risk the unintentional consequence of communicating that God works only in the service event and not in our daily lives."

He cautioned, "If you don't take these opportunities to talk with your kids seriously, you are a poor steward. But be warned ... if you do, they will challenge you at some pretty deep levels. Processing mission trips with our kids has meant taking a hard look at our family budget and how we spend our money, our choice of where to live, what church activities become a priority, and whether the Lord wanted us to open our family up to foster care and/or adoption. It has meant sending a child overseas in between high school and college, eliminating the opportunity for some scholarship aid. It has changed the college dreams of one child as he has wrestled seriously with the debt and accompanying restrictions incurred by an expensive private school and God's call on his life. As parents, it has meant continuing to grow in our own engagement with these issues and not allowing ourselves to believe that we have arrived at an understanding of how to live out the heart of God in our culture."

This family takes seriously their responsibility to process mission trips with their kids. We're inspired by them, and we hope you are too.

Develop Ongoing Relationships with Those You Serve

Viewing justice as a sticky before/during/after process also allows your family to develop real and ongoing relationships with people of different cultures and socioeconomic statuses.

One family shared their story of engaging their kids at a young age in relationships with kids in poverty. What started as participation in a simple Christmas outreach turned into long-term engagement with members of a community in Baja, Mexico. When Cal and Hayley saw their church was going to support families in Mexico through supplying Christmas gift boxes, they picked up a photo of a girl named

Karina, who is the same age as their daughter Sofia. Sofia was just two at the time, but the family decided not only to donate the requested gift box but also to keep praying for Karina throughout the next year. Sofia often reminded her parents to pray for Karina and made sure the family kept her picture in a prominent place.

Two years later, Cal and Hayley's church publicized a trip to the same church in Mexico, to deliver Christmas boxes and to serve in the church and community over a long weekend. Cal and Hayley decided to take their family (which now included another daughter) along on this churchwide trip. Based on a foundation of two years of prayer with Sofia, this trip opened up the possibility that their family would actually meet Karina and her family. As it turned out, Karina was not only still part of the small community but actually lived across the dirt street from the church. Sofia was delighted to meet and get to play with the friend she had been praying for with her parents, and Cal and Hayley were also able to meet and befriend Karina's parents (with the help of a good translator). Gifts were exchanged both ways as Karina's mom shared candy from her small roadside stand with the visiting kids.

This was the beginning of a relationship that has continued over many years. The family continues to support their church's ongoing relationship with the church in Mexico, and as often as possible they participate in church trips to the community where they again connect with Karina and her family. In fact, Cal and Hayley now run the Christmas box outreach with help from their kids. In between trips they send letters, photos, and kids' artwork back and forth with Karina. Cal and Hayley have discovered that their relationships with Karina and her family, as well as the local husband-wife pastor team and their family, have shaped their children's perspectives on poverty, materialism, and cross-cultural relationships. In fact, they point to their involvement in Mexico as one of the most significant markers in their family's spiritual journey. In their dining room hangs a photo of their children playing with Karina as a tangible reminder of the ways their everyday decisions as a family impact the lives and faith of people around the world, and specifically those of their friends in Mexico.

Make Justice Part of Everyday Life

Many (maybe even most) teenagers will show way more enthusiasm for rescuing a girl from Haiti or visiting Honduras than they will for turning off their lights to save electricity or for being more kind to the homeless guy they pass every day on the way to school (both of which are also justice issues). What can you do with your kids to help them live out justice in their everyday decisions?

One family at our church has decided to serve by making their home a safe place for other kids. The two teenage daughters know that they can bring friends home, whether they are friends who want to have fun (the parents make sure to have lots of snacks on hand) or friends who need to talk. If the latter, the parents, Jackson and LaRosa, rearrange their work schedules so that they can sit on their living room couches and lend a listening ear. LaRosa reports that their daughters seem more comfortable talking with them about their struggles when they see their friends sitting on their sofas and doing so too.

While the girls were in middle school, Jackson noticed that Sam, one of the guys who came over regularly, was starting to party and hang out with gangbangers. Jackson is a police officer, so he decided to take Sam under his wing and give him a tour of local gang sites and the nearby jail. During the tour, Jackson warned him, "This is where your life is heading. Is this what you want?" Realizing it wasn't, Sam chose the narrow path of life instead of the wide path of destruction. Six years later, Jackson is still mentoring Sam as he pursues a job as a firefighter.

Feeling called to make a difference in the local public high school, another couple I know has mobilized their family to change that school's climate. Just before their oldest entered ninth grade, Tim and Kathy learned that the school's test scores were so low that it was on the brink of being taken over by the state of California.

Desperate for help and input, the new school principal held a series of summer town-hall meetings. One of the top needs emerging from those meetings was the school's physical environment. The drab exterior of the school was sending a sad message to kids: we don't care much about this school, so you don't need to either. The entire campus needed a face-lift.

Tim and Kathy volunteered to fix up the school over the summer so that when students, including their own daughter, showed up that fall, they would know the school was now on the path to success. Thanks to donations of two thousand people hours as well as $75,000 worth of paint and greenery, Tim and Kathy accomplished their goal, and the students—including their daughter—knew something was different that September.

Since then, Tim and Kathy have served on the school site council, created weekly email notices in both English and Spanish for parents, and worked to secure funding for a part-time outreach coordinator at the school. But even more important, they have built relationships — usually cross-cultural relationships — with other kids and families.

Upon hearing that one of their kids' friends who lived with his mom and brother was being evicted, Tim and Kathy asked their kids if it would be all right for this struggling family of three to move in with them. The kids agreed it would be, and the threesome moved into their living room. Unbeknownst to Tim and Kathy, the mom had terminal cancer and had only a few months to live.

Over the next five months, this mom's body was taken over by cancer to the point, Kathy recalls, that "she basically just lay on our couch, groaning all day. Our kids saw that; they saw us care for a dying woman on our couch." Those memories stuck with the kids and showed them the power of serving someone in their ultimate time of need.

This family's unpaid, part-time devotion to the school has come at a price. Both self-employed, Tim and Kathy have devoted hours that could have been funneled into their business. While their kids have for the most part been supportive, they have at times grumbled about their parents' busyness. Perhaps hardest of all, Tim and Kathy have understandably wondered if a school with more resources would be not just easier but better for their kids.

But then they think of their son, Luke. Luke is now a college student who is majoring in elementary education and African-American studies because he wants to be a teacher in an inner-city school. As with all of their kids, Luke's faith was shaped by the family's commitment to live out Sticky Justice every day. Kathy summarizes, "There has been much pain, but there has also been much, much joy."

Guide Your Kids toward Caring

You may be reading this chapter and thinking to yourself, "All these ideas work when your kids care about the world around them. My kids seem so self-absorbed. What do I do with my kids when they don't seem to care?"

The most important thing to remember is that even more important than how deeply or even actively our kids care now is that their faith *eventually* moves toward justice as a core and expressed value. Adolescents are by nature somewhat self-absorbed. Our role, then, is to help our kids move in a steady and direct path toward caring for others.

Our best shot at helping our kids in this is by modeling our own care for others—not just the poor but also the different, the hurting, and the weak. How we talk about others, even those who don't necessarily "deserve" our care, says a lot to our kids about our understanding of Jesus' message about loving others.

With our own kids, Chap and I (along with our spouses) try to do two things: First, we pray and serve others together as a family as much and as often as we can. Second, we take every chance we can to get our kids out there on the front lines of mercy, justice, and service. We strongly believe that the more our children can come alongside those who are poor, broken, or weak, the more they will recognize how much the "least of these" have to teach those of us who think we are rich, whole, and strong. Over time, community builds compassion.

Be Creative in Your Pursuit of Justice

Recently I presented our research findings about Sticky Justice to a gathering of parents at a family camp. When I asked parents to share their own creative ways to engage their kids in justice, one dad offered that he keeps an envelope in his wallet with some cash in it. His wife does the same in her purse. Their kids know this, and they've decided as a family that the cash goes to people in need. Their job is to be on the lookout for folks who could use a bit of help. After they find someone and agree to give them the money, the family replenishes the envelopes and remains on the lookout.

Another family wanted to instill in their kids a vision for generous and sacrificial giving. Instead of pocketing the profits from their Saturday yard sale, they gave every cent to an international missions organization. When others heard about this yard sale, they donated some of their belongings too. The family worked hard together all Saturday, knowing that children in Africa would be the ultimate beneficiaries of their labor.

Priceless. I love the creativity of families when it comes to justice. They are sticking with it.

sticky reflection and discussion questions

1. How do you think your kids would fill in the blank of what being part of your family means? What would you want them to say?

2. How would you define the difference between *service* and *justice*?

3. When has a service experience not produced the spiritual "bang for the buck" you hoped for and expected?

4. Think about the next time your kids will be doing something to serve others. What could you do before the event to help prepare them for what they will face? What could you do afterward?

5. Think about a few things your kids love or are good at. How can you help them connect their areas of interest with their skills and creativity to pursue justice in some area?

7

a sticky bridge out of home

I wish there was more of a transition.
It seemed like when I was done with high school,
everything ended really fast.
—Joel

I didn't think I really needed to go to church
to be a strong Christian, but after being away from
church completely while I studied abroad,
I went back to church one Sunday and saw people
caring for each other in a way that I had not
experienced outside of the church body.
—Anna-Maria

There's no place better on a warm summer day than the beach. So thought Mary Ann, a sixty-five-year-old friend of our (Kara's) family, who decided to take advantage of a marvelous Thursday in July to go to the beach with her father, who was in his late eighties.

Mary Ann was enjoying the waves in shoulder-deep water when she noticed her father waving wildly on the beach. He was gesturing frantically, beckoning her back to the shore.

Fearing something was wrong with her father, Mary Ann hustled as quickly as she could into shallower waters and then onto the sand. She ran up to the beach blanket where her father was sitting and through her hard breathing asked, "Dad, are you okay? What's wrong?"

"Oh, nothing," he replied. "I just thought you were out a little bit far."

Once a parent, always a parent.

Even after our kids graduate, they are still our kids.

And yet our kids someday become adults too.

This transition from childhood to adulthood is significant in part because it's such a liminal (in-between) period of time.[1] As they graduate, your kids are moving out of one world but are not quite yet in another, so by definition (of anthropologists, anyway), they are in a liminal period. They stand on a threshold, having largely stepped away from their old identity but just starting to open the door to their next stage of life and new identity. Your son or daughter knows on some level that this is happening but often has very little guidance for how to live in the in-between world or how to step through the door into post–high school emerging adulthood.

So how do you help your child build a sticky bridge out of the home? How can we prepare our kids—especially those getting close to high school graduation—for all they'll encounter when "Pomp and Circumstance" fades? And as our kids are transitioning out of high school, what sorts of transitions do we need to make in our relationships with them so that our entire family emerges with stickier faith?[2]

Sticky Findings

Most Kids Do Not Feel Prepared for College

Unfortunately, only one in seven graduating seniors feels "very prepared" for what college brings their way. According to students themselves, most don't feel set up for success in the transition to college. This is especially tragic given our research showing that feeling prepared matters. The more students feel prepared—whether it be to find a church, engage in a ministry, make friends, or handle new choices about alcohol, sex, and parties—the more likely their faith is to grow.

The First Two Weeks of College Set the Trajectory

Over and over, students have told us that the first two weeks at college are when they make key decisions about drinking and other high-risk behaviors, right along with choosing whether to go to church or to a campus ministry. Many of these decisions are influenced by the new friends freshmen surround themselves with and the situations in which they put themselves. Most kids are unprepared for the intensity of those first days and weeks and have no strategy for how to make decisions during that critical time.

> *Don't skip church that first week, because it just makes it easier to skip it the second week and then the eighth week....*
> —Young Mi

Finding and Connecting to a Church Is Difficult

Engaging in a church or campus group during the freshman year makes a big difference, but most students don't know how to find a church in college. Though nearly every parent hopes their kids will get involved with a church during college, fewer than 40 percent of students feel prepared to find a new church. Not surprisingly, finding a church was one of the top three most difficult parts of the transition.

> Never let your son or daughter leave without a few leads for potential churches or campus ministries to check out. For help connecting with other incoming Christian freshmen and learning about campus ministries, point your child to liveabove.com, hosted by the Youth Transition Network.

For kids living away from home, getting connected in either an off-campus church or on-campus Christian fellowship is linked with Sticky Faith in their freshman year. Yet during the fall of freshman year, only 40 percent of youth group alum were attending an on-campus fellowship once a week or more and 57 percent were attending church once a week or more.

Managing Daily Life Is a Major Challenge

Managing daily life is overwhelming for most college students, leaving no time or energy to think about faith. In his study of college freshmen, sociologist Tim Clydesdale found that students become all-consumed with the game he calls "daily life management." Facing the sudden instability of their new environment, schedule, and virtually limitless boundaries, operating from day to day becomes a practice of sheer survival. Clydesdale describes college students' new juggling act this way: "[T]hey manage their personal relationships—with romantic partners, friends, and authority figures; they manage personal gratifications—including substance use and sexual activity; and they manage their economic lives—with its expanding necessities and rising lifestyle expectations."[3]

Our research seems to confirm this. During their freshman year, nearly half of students in our study felt anxious that so much was suddenly up to them to decide. We also found that students struggle most to integrate their faith with their handling of time and money.

Yet both tend to be big hang-ups in college. Given that the average credit-card debt of a college student is more than $3,000 and half of undergraduates own four or more credit cards,[4] these are areas where our kids need help thinking harder about reality. As one college student shared with us, "In high school, *everything* was scheduled. In college, I was finished with classes by noon, and had all day to do whatever I wanted. And no one asks you if you went to class or

Compared to high school, I now know more about myself and less about what I believe than I used to. I hope this will resolve at some point in my life ... at this point it's on hold because I don't have the time or the tools. It's hard to find time to think about religion or God, and college feels more like living from one day to the next and losing focus on big-picture things.

—Conner

did your homework. I had to learn how to manage my own time well."

Advice from College Students to Seniors

When we asked college students what they would share with a group of high school seniors about going to college, their answers clustered into the following categories, listed in order of importance:

1. Find a faith community at college and get connected.
2. Engage with your faith, including emerging questions and doubts.
3. Be prepared to be challenged.
4. Practice personal spiritual disciplines.

Contact with Parents Helps Kids

Parents who think they need to go "radio silent" when their kids go to college are actually doing their kids a disservice. In our study, contact with parents—whether by phone, email, or text—is related to practical and emotional adjustment to college. This was true regardless of who made the contact.

Sticky Faith Made Practical

You don't have control over many of your graduating child's decisions, but you do have control over how you relate to your child. How do you strike a balance between recognizing your son or daughter is transitioning into a new chapter of growing independence and still an involved parent? It's not an easy dance, to be sure, but following a few simple steps will make the dance easier and more fun — for both you and your child.

Trust God with Your Child

This is so important we're going to say it again: trust God with your child.

In chapter 2, we reframed the Sticky Gospel as a whole-hearted trust in the God who is entirely trustworthy. There is no better time for you to live out the power of that gospel than as your own child is moving into a new phase of life.

In my (Chap's) and my wife's experience, trusting God with our children looks different at different stages of their development. Trusting God with our children was easier when our kids were younger. At that stage, we needed to be more direct and controlling in order to be good shepherds and stewards of our kids' lives and choices.

When our daughter was in sixth grade, for example, we were concerned with a particular friendship she was developing. She wanted to travel for the weekend with this friend's family. We had a hard time with this invitation because we were concerned about what could happen if she went with them. The dilemma we faced was whether to trust God with our daughter and let her go, even though we were concerned about what could happen, or to protect her (in love) by saying she could not go with this family for the weekend. We decided to let her go, but we worked hard to stay close to the other family, checked in with our daughter, and kept our eyes on the overall relationship.

When our kids grew older, we had no choice but to trust that God cared for our children, simply because we had less ability to control their friendships, behaviors, and life choices than we did when they were young. We had always believed that God loves our kids more than even we do, and when they were in high school and beyond, we were forced to live this out.

Regardless of your son or daughter's age, it is your job both to make sure that they are reasonably protected *as well as* to give them the space to roam into adulthood. Trusting God with your child means that while you are still his chosen representative to your kid, you rest knowing that it is God's power and mercy that will protect them over the long haul.

Let Your Child Know Your Unconditional Love

You might think you've been telling them that you love them all these years, but has your message gotten through? And do they know that you love them *unconditionally* (or at least as close to unconditionally as humanly possible)?

Why is showing unconditional love so important as your child is graduating? As great as your adjustment is to having a high school graduate, theirs is even greater. As they graduate, they step into a host of potential new arenas— new school, new job, new friends, new dating potential, new church, new place to live. Every new arena is a new opportunity for them to fail.

Some of your children will recognize this potential for failure ahead of time and express their fears and misgivings to you. When they do, reassure them of their skills, the power of their hard work, and the unconditional love of God and yourself.

When your children do step out and fail, do they know that you will still support and love them unconditionally? One youth worker friend of mine (Kara's), Danny, faced this question head-on when he received a 2:00 a.m. phone call from one of his high school seniors. Just as when you're a parent, when you're a youth leader, 2:00 a.m. phone calls from kids are never good.

This one was no exception. On the other end of the line was one of Danny's male students who confessed to Danny, "I just slept with my girlfriend." His girlfriend was also part of the youth ministry.

Danny's heart started pounding as he offered to meet with the student for breakfast that morning.

Next, Danny did what you would have done, which was pray a lot and sleep only a little. When Danny showed up for breakfast, the kid was already sitting at the restaurant table. Danny started to express how much he loved him, and that God loved him, and that it is God's kindness that leads us to repentance (see Rom. 2:4).

> *My parents have always encouraged me to look at what I believe and question why I believe it, knowing that this will strengthen my faith and my conviction. They have always been open and accepting of what I believe, and by challenging me to discover why I believe what I believe, they have fostered a strong faith built on knowledge and study, rather than a weak one built on doing what everyone else is doing.*
>
> —Desiree

The high school kid stopped Danny before he got much farther. "Actually, I didn't sleep with my girlfriend. I just wanted to see how you would respond to me if I had."

Now that kid needs therapy.

But I would guess that most—and maybe all—of our children are in more subtle ways wondering if we can handle their failures. Every time our children share their struggles with us, we have the opportunity to pair their need to confess their sin with the freedom that comes from trusting God. It's all the better when that confession and freedom are wrapped in a blanket of our own verbal affirmation of God's never-stopping love.

And when your students succeed in these new arenas—which they will at times—how do you celebrate with them? Do you simply applaud their results, or do you congratulate them on their hard work and then remind them, "Even if you had failed, I still would love you the same"?

Don't Do for Your Child
What They Can Do for Themselves

You've likely heard of "helicopter parents," parents who hover over their children, including their new college students, often smothering both their children and bystanders. Or perhaps you've heard of "velcro parents," who are attached to their son or daughter. These velcro or helicopter parents have notoriously called their college student's professor when their daughter received an unsatisfactory grade or emailed potential employers to sing the praises of their son.

Whether motivated by their own sense of guilt or fear of their child's (and vicariously their own) failure, helicopter parents have forgotten a lesson that many of us tried to follow when our children were young: don't do for a child what they can do for themselves. When your daughter was five, you let her tie her own shoelaces, even though it took so long and it was painful to watch. When your son was twelve, you encouraged him to finish his own science project, even though you knew you could have stepped in and made a much slicker water-evaporation display board.

Now that they are eighteen, you need to stand back and let them try their own adventures and make their own mistakes. Sure, you can help them come up with a road map (which we'll discuss later in this chapter). But it's up to them to follow that map and reach the destination. Your job is to support them and heap unconditional love on them; their job is to sit in the driver's seat of their own lives.

Give Your Child New Freedom

Many parents whose children stay at home after graduation make the mistake of thinking that since the kids still live at home, they need to follow the exact same rules. While it's widely recognized that adolescence is lengthening and that high school graduation doesn't mark a definitive transition into adulthood anymore, high school graduation does nonetheless mark entry into a new phase called "emerging adulthood."

> For more on the lengthening of adolescence and late adolescence, see *www.stickyfaith.org*.

Emerging adulthood, like its precursors of early and late adolescence, is marked by a need for boundaries, but those boundaries can—and should—be widened. This means it's time for a later curfew, and it's time for you to ask fewer questions about when they're going to find time to study for midterms. We hope you've been giving your child a developmentally appropriate growing voice and even negotiating power throughout childhood and adolescence so that they learn to think and act for themselves. Emerging adulthood is a time when you allow your son or daughter even more freedom so that they can fully stretch their wings.

Prepare Your Child for College

This section is meant to be intensely practical, a catalogue of ideas for your ongoing use as you prayerfully help your son or daughter transition from high school to college.

Visit a Variety of Churches

This may seem counterintuitive to some of us, but given how challenging it is for college students to find churches, we encourage you to pull your son or daughter out of your own church. No, you're not ditching church to grab donuts. You're using the time to visit a handful of other churches, perhaps on Sundays during the summer after graduation.

> *The longer you wait, the harder it is to get plugged in to a church or a campus ministry.*
> —Glyn

As you travel together to different churches, worship with different congregations, and debrief afterward, your child will begin to think through what is important to them as they search for a new church away from home. It also raises great questions about why churches and denominations are different and what those differences mean. If you start before colleges take their summer break, you could also visit some college campus ministries.

The point of visiting different churches or college groups is not to glamorize "church shopping" but to prayerfully and thoughtfully help your child grasp what it's like to visit new churches. Here are some questions to help your child analyze their experience at different churches:

1. What is the mission or vision of this group?
2. What is the theological heritage of this group?
3. Where does this group meet? How am I going to get there?
4. Are there folks I know who might want to come with me to this group? How important is that to me?
5. When does this group meet? How does that fit my schedule?
6. How many people are involved? Of those who are involved, how many people are my gender and/or year in school and/or ethnicity? How important are those similarities or differences to me?

> When we asked college students what criteria were most important to them in choosing a church, these were their top five, in order of importance:
>
> 1. The teaching
> 2. The mission or vision
> 3. The leaders
> 4. The worship
> 5. The outreach to people in need

7. Who leads this group? How do I connect with the leaders?
8. What's the teaching like? How about the worship?
9. Are there small groups or Bible studies?
10. What does this group do to reach out to people who don't know Jesus yet?

11. What does this group do to help those who are poor or marginalized?

12. How can I use my gifts and talents in this group?

Think about Spiritual Life When You Visit Colleges

While you're visiting colleges, help your son or daughter think about what faith might look like at that college. What can you find out about spiritual life while you're there? What campus ministries exist, and can you meet with leaders as part of your visit? If there are chapel services, try to attend one. While you're at it, take the opportunity to visit a church or two near each campus too.

Talk about Life after High School

Whether it's an arranged time to chat or a conversation that comes up as you're grabbing a quick breakfast together, we hope you'll have many opportunities to talk with your child about life after high school. The list of conversation topics below is a culmination of research, think tanks, and feedback from youth leaders and parents across the country (listed in no particular order). Start thinking now about what your son or daughter needs to discuss, and choose three or four topics from this list to get the ball rolling.

Finding a new church and campus ministry

Finding new friends, especially new Christian relationships

Navigating old friendships, which often change rapidly after high school

Recovering after you stumble, fall down, or run the other way from Christ

Managing time

Managing money

Handling emerging doubts and questions about faith

Engaging your changing view of God, yourself, and others

Staying in touch with adults from your home church

Finding new mentors

Managing changing relationships with parents and other family members

Practicing faith in college (spiritual disciplines and other practices)

Exploring and building your faith identity as opposed to lockboxing your faith away (see chapter 3)

Having conversations with students from other faiths and worldviews

Recognizing and using your gifts and talents to serve others

Discerning vocation and calling

Pursuing missional living on the college campus and in adult life

Developing critical thinking and decision-making skills

Understanding the Sticky Gospel (chapter 2) and living under God's grace

Preparing for dating relationships in college

Preparing for the possibility of finding a marriage partner during or after college

Prepare for Loss

One of the hallmarks of the freshman experience is loss, and often students are surprised by this feeling. Help prepare your child for losses they may face by talking through the following types of loss:

Material loss. "Yes, you can grieve if you lose your cell phone."

Relationship loss. "Yes, you can grieve if you break up with your boyfriend."

Loss of a dream. "Yes, you can grieve not getting into the college you wanted."

Functional loss. "Yes, you can grieve breaking your arm."

Role loss. "Yes, you can grieve no longer being a high school student."

Systemic loss. "Yes, you can grieve when you leave home and your entire network of supportive relationships to go away to school."[5]

> For more resources on loss,
> visit *www.stickyfaith.org.*

Talk about Time and Money

Based on what we've heard from college students, we want to call your attention to two topics on the previous list: managing time and money. College students face new temptations in spending their time and money, so you need to make a special effort to help your child come up with a plan for how they will wisely use both. Work up a budget with them. Develop a feasible schedule that includes classes, homework, job, church, and enough time with friends. If you haven't already, now is a good time for you to share your own calendar and family budget so they see how you try to wisely steward your time and money.

Create a Two-Week Plan

Given our research showing that the first two weeks set a trajectory for the rest of college, create a "first two-week plan" with your child. When will they go to church? When will they study? When will they connect with family? When will they get time with friends? What will they do those first Thursday, Friday, and Saturday evenings? They can always deviate from the plan, but at least they've got a Sticky Faith road map as they start their journey.

Celebrate a Few "Lasts" Together

During and after graduation, your child is savoring a host of "lasts" with their friends—the last day hanging out at the mall, the last movie they'll see together, and the last late-night hamburger at their favorite hangout. They are so busy with their friends that they might not have the relational energy to appreciate the "lasts" with their family too.

Without being maudlin or overly specific (e.g., this is the last Wednesday morning you'll have chocolate chip pancakes), in the final weeks of your child's time at home, celebrate a few "lasts" together. Give your son a few bucks to take his siblings out for ice cream. Encourage your daughter to swing by her favorite aunt's house on her way home from work. Go out for a final family dinner at your child's favorite restaurant. These mini-rituals can help bring a sense of closure for your child and your entire family. You might want to talk with your son or daughter a few weeks ahead of time to get a sense of how they'd like to spend the last few weeks, and coordinate plans so they have adequate time for good-byes with friends (which will likely feel more important to them right now).

Process Your Empty-Nest Emotions

The "empty nest" (or at least emptying nest, if you have other kids at home) gives you and your spouse much to celebrate — more freedom and fewer day-to-day responsibilities. But many parents also experience grief, as well as doubt about whether they did all they could to prepare their graduate.

We hope this book will help alleviate many of those doubts, but nonetheless you will probably need some time with your spouse and other close friends to share your thoughts and feelings. You might also consider finding a new channel for the time and energy you have poured into parenting your son or daughter through high school. Perhaps there's a new ministry opportunity, or another high school kid in your church or neighborhood who could use some time with you.

Prepare for the Transition through Group or Church Events

The following ideas can help your son or daughter realize they are not alone as they turn the corner from high school to college. Whether it's with your church or with a few of your child's closest friends, one or two of these group events might form the adhesive of your child's Sticky Faith. While some of these ideas assume the involvement of a youth leader, you or another parent can fill those shoes when needed.

Plan Periodic Senior Gatherings

This is probably the idea we've heard the most, with all kinds of variations on the theme. Here are a few tips for making these gatherings successful:

Start early. Some churches and groups tell us they've moved from a few meetings in late spring to a yearlong series beginning in the fall of students' senior year.

Invite the senior pastor, or even have dinner at his or her home.

Culminate the series with an overnighter or a meaningful trip together (from camping to mission work to Disneyland).

Host gender-separate groups for some or all of your meetings, focusing on some of the same issues but also exploring special considerations guys and girls need to make as they prepare for life after high school. For instance, how will they handle romantic relationships and sexual pressure in the midst of the college hookup scene? How do same-gender friendships look different in college for guys and for girls than they do in high school? What does it mean to be a man or woman of God, and how do gender roles they've learned or assumed in the past fit—or not—with their current understanding?

Invite your church's college pastor or other campus pastors or campus ministry leaders to come speak to seniors. Ask former youth group grads who have made it through the freshman year to come share with your seniors. Invite college students from different perspectives: those from both secular and Christian campuses, those who join fraternities or sororities and those who don't, those who get connected with campus ministries and those who don't, and so on.

> As a follow-up to our research, we've also developed a Sticky Faith senior curriculum as part of this line of resources. You might want to get a copy for your church's youth pastor and maybe one for yourself too. You can order it at *www.stickyfaith.org*.

Create Mentoring Partnerships

One church we know pairs high school seniors with adult mentors from the congregation with the expectation that they will continue the mentoring relationship through at least the first year after high school. Another idea is to connect seniors in high school with senior adults in the congregation, either as short-term conversation partners or long-term mentors. Or you could help your son or daughter connect with an adult in a vocational path that your child hopes to pursue.

> The Evangelical Covenant denomination has created a free mentoring guide for young adults and their mentors called "The Real Life Field Guide." You can download this discussion-rich tool for free at:
>
> *www.covchurch.org/resources/real-life-field-guide/*.

Transition into Servant Leadership

If your son or daughter isn't involved yet in a servant leadership role at your church, before or after graduation is a good time for him or her to help out in your church's middle school or elementary ministry. This usually works best when your child is teamed with and supported by adult leaders during their service.

Celebrate Seniors in a Worship Service

Many churches already have some kind of "Senior Sunday" recognition service. Sometimes this consists of parading students across the platform and giving them Bibles. Other times there's more involved. Here are a few ideas to help your Senior Sunday get stickier.

Invite seniors to share with the congregation not just where they're headed next but also their stories of faith and the ways they have been shaped to this point by the congregation and youth ministry.

Allow seniors to take over the service, crafting and leading the worship and sharing the teaching. If it is acceptable in your context, empower seniors to serve communion elements to the congregation.

Incorporate ritual acts of blessing, such as the congregation speaking a blessing liturgy and/or laying hands on students in prayer.

Publicly acknowledge and pray for seniors at the beginning *and* end of their senior year. The beginning of the year can serve as a commissioning for the transitional period ahead, and the end of the year can be a time of conferring adulthood and commissioning for service.

Involve parents by inviting them to the platform to pray

for their kids, or giving them a chance to publicly share advice they would give to parents of younger children. Mentors, small group leaders, and other significant adults from the church could also join in this time to surround students with prayer.

Celebrate a "Senior *Barak*"

Barak is the Hebrew word for "bless," and a church near Fuller Seminary in Pasadena holds a yearly tradition of a *barak* night for friends, family, and youth leaders to bless graduating seniors. Each student's parents are given an information sheet about a month before the event, including instructions for writing a letter of blessing to their child. Parents read the letter they have written out loud in front of the group. Then other students, leaders, and family have opportunities to share. As one student reflected, "Usually it's hard to get encouragement from my dad, so to hear him read a letter to me was powerful."

> To download an instruction sheet for a Senior *Barak* or to find more ideas on creating rites of passage for seniors, visit *www.stickyfaith.org*.

Connect with Other Parents

Consider hosting a parents-of-seniors small group that meets one or more times, or a workshop or prayer night for other parents. We know of one church that gathers parents in one room to make a list of what they think their kids need to know before they leave home, while students gather in a nearby room to make their own list of what they think they need to know. Then the two groups share their lists and have rich conversation about the similarities and differences.

Letters from College

In our surveys and interviews, we asked college students to think back from the vantage point of three or four years out and consider what they would say now to a group of high school seniors about preparing for the transition. Parts of their responses are scattered throughout this book, but we pulled together a few particularly powerful quotes to share as we close this chapter.

> *I would tell them to prepare, to plan ahead. When you go away to college, you don't just say, "I'm going to leave, I want to go here," and just pack your bag and go. You learn about it, you find out what the environment is going to be like, if you're going to need furniture in your dorm, and what kind of clothes you're going to need to prepare for the weather. If you're going to do that amount of preparing for moving, your faith needs the same kind of preparation. Look into what the college environment is going to provide for you positively, and maybe expose you to negatively, and prepare for all of that. Know your faith and be willing and strong enough to let it be challenged.*
>
> —Luke

> *College is also one of the neatest times to be bold enough to share your faith because I think the potential for impact on a college campus is enormous.*
>
> —Allie

It's easy to be naïve and think that because you were a strong Christian and knew what you believed and why you believed it in high school, that it's going to be the same in college. It's not! In high school I had a great community, but coming to college is so testing. And man, it can be so lonely that you start to question everything. So get plugged in with people who care about you, at all levels. That would have been so helpful for me, and I don't think I would be feeling so lost about stuff right now.

—Zachary

It's okay to go through periods of doubt and distrust and disillusionment. It's okay to go through periods of questioning and confusion. Don't run away from them. At the same time, don't go off the deep end. Do the intellectual and spiritual soul searching within the context of a secure community of people who truly love you.

—Sophia

If anyone is going into college saying, "I want to know how best to honor God in this situation that I'm going into," they can succeed. I don't think that anyone who goes through life looking for opportunities to honor God will be left hanging. I think God is faithful to answer that and to say, "You're looking for me, and I'm going to reveal myself to you."

—Neil

sticky reflection and discussion questions

1. How are you feeling about the reality that your child is graduating? What are you most grateful to God for? What causes you fear or misgivings?

2. What does it look like to trust God with your son or daughter as he or she is graduating?

3. Do you think your child *really* knows that you love them unconditionally? How could you handle their next failure or success in such a way that you shower them with unconditional love?

4. What family and group or church events would you like to try with your child? When is the best time to try them? Who else could you partner with (other parents, mentors, small group leader, youth leader) to help prepare your child for the transition?

the ups and downs
of the sticky faith journey

*Your faith is your faith. It is not your parents' or your
pastor's or your friends'. You need to know what you
believe and why you believe it, not so you can justify it
to other people but so you can justify it to yourself . . .
so you can live without internal contradictions.*
—Devon

*You definitely have to be confident that you have made
the decision to follow Christ and have personal reasons.
"Because my parents are Christian" or "My youth
group leader said so" simply don't work anymore.*
—Tara

By now you might be thinking—and hoping—that if you
just follow this book's research-based recommendations,
you'll have a guaranteed plan for Sticky Faith.

Sorry. We can't make any such guarantees.

This last chapter deals with the uncomfortable truth that
the Sticky Faith journey is full of both ups and downs. While
we hope and pray that our sons and daughters remain glued

to Jesus, they may wander from faith, at least for a season. Not all kids drift from the faith of their parents, but at one time or another, many kids do, at least for a while. In fact, we would say that you ought to count on it. Hold fast to the idea that there are healthy elements to drifting, and be humbly grateful if you happen to be one of those whose kids stayed true and faithful to the gospel as they transitioned from adolescence to adulthood.

Funny thing, drifting. The word conjures up an image of floating on a raft in calm waters or down a lazy river, without direction or propulsion. Drifting evokes pictures of wandering without motivation. To many parents, this is an apt picture of what adolescents experience when they jump overboard from their parents' well-appointed and well-maintained faith yacht.

One of the many nice things for me (Chap) about getting older (and there are lots more things than they tell you!) and having older kids is that life is a great teacher. There is plenty of information about parenting available, and lots of advice, and long lists of "guiding principles." But when all is said and done, life is anything but a straight line, or to stay with the water metaphor, a calm canal. It is instead a wild river, full of both turbulent waters and hidden rocks. When your teenager rides that river, what seems like drifting may in fact be a natural faith course that, while different than your own, may still eventually help your kids stick with Jesus.

Sticky Findings

Children Need to Own Their Faith

Ultimately, you want your child's faith journey to lead to just that: your *child's* faith. At some point, every parent wakes up to the realization that what matters to and for our kids are not *our* hopes, plans, and dreams for them, but rather *their* hopes, plans, and dreams. This applies to sports, music, drama, and dance. It applies to academic interests. And perhaps even more so, it applies to their faith.

When our three kids were young, we were diligent to pray for and with them. We rejoiced over the most intricate details of any and every expression of their connection with Jesus. We tape-recorded early prayers, and we've kept their Sunday school finger paintings of biblical heroes. As they went through elementary school and went to vacation Bible school and day camp and finally a trip to the "big kids' camp" at Forest Home Conference Center near us, we cherished every excited gush of what they did, what they sang, and what God had done in their lives.

In middle school, the faith journey becomes a bit dicier. One week our kids would love their small group leader and youth group, the next week it was "boring." Their church and youth group experience revolved around what they were going to do while they were there. In middle school, church was still an extension of us. And therefore, so was faith.

Once they hit high school, and especially college, the game changed—dramatically.

In contrast to early adolescence, in high school the question is not so much "What are we going to do?" but "Who is going to be there?" The shared experience with peers, and especially the opposite sex, was a big motivation for our kids in high school. This coincided with the beginning of our kids' movement away from our parental faith into a place where it was safe for them to explore their own faith.

Our experience as a family mirrors the research we've presented in this book: by the time your child enters late adolescence, your faith is no longer what sustains them, or even holds their interest in God or church. As they mentally move into abstract awareness and begin to reflectively wrestle with their identity, they realize that Christianity is something they need to discover and decide to embrace on their own.

Children Who Experience Unconditional Support Are More Likely to Have Sticky Faith

For today's kids, feelings of isolation, performance-driven agendas, and abandonment by those who are supposed to be there for them have taken a massive toll. It is not that some have been abandoned and therefore only those "fringe" kids feel the effects of growing up without the social support needed to navigate life's challenges and expectations. Rather, as a result of growing up in our fast-paced, fragmented, and externally focused culture, kids have lost "social capital," that sense that there are at least a handful of adults who care and are willing to pour themselves into their lives without a self-serving agenda. At some level for all kids, growing up is difficult and lonely.

Into this reality we add our own desire and expectation that our children grow up as faithful and consistent followers of Jesus. We don't mean this to be another high bar for our kids to have to reach, but because for most of us it is such a highly sacred value, it is difficult to stand back and dispassionately allow our kids to make their own choices. By the very nature of faith commitment, we as parents naturally desire (usually with deep and vocal passion) for our kids to follow in our faith footsteps.

Your kids know this. It is never far off their developmental desktop. The dilemma our kids face as they move into high school and beyond is they know how much we want them to take their faith seriously. But they also soon come to know that faith is ultimately meaningless unless they choose it for themselves. This tension can cause a number of responses, from both parent and child, as kids begin to explore their own faith. Kids will do everything, from keeping silent about their thoughts, to lying or pretending to be leaning in their parents' direction, to getting fed up with the pressure (however implicit and subtle it may seem to you as the parent) until they don't care anymore and faith doesn't matter to them.

When the daughter of good friends went through a difficult patch during high school and beyond, they worked hard to find the balance between tough love and encouragement. During her senior year, she not only pulled away from her faith, but she also pulled away from school, friends, and family. She told her folks she loved them, but her deceit, attitude, and behavior were very destructive and caused her parents great pain.

One afternoon after a particularly bad week, I asked her dad how he could handle her, and if he wasn't just flat-out disgusted with her. He didn't answer but motioned me to follow him upstairs into his study. He picked up a framed letter that was sitting in the center of his desk. Without saying a word, he let me know what his daughter meant to him:

Daughter 17

I have a daughter 17
When she lies to me ... I love her.
When she disappoints me ... I love her.
When she doesn't live up to my expectations ... I love her.
When she reflects poorly on my name ... I love her.
"Now I can understand how when she pleases you ...
    and obeys
you ... and fulfills you ...," you say.
But that's not what I'm talking about.
It's when she does none of these things ... I love her
AND for a very simple reason:
I'm her father ... and she's my child.

When your kids disappoint you (note I said *when*, not *if*), you may be tempted to distance yourself from them to teach them a lesson or maybe even to protect yourself. Everywhere they turn, your kids have grown up in a culture in which when they struggle or fail, people tend to walk away. Especially during their lowest times, your kids need to know that, above all else, you are there for them, regardless of what they are going through.

In the case of my friends, their daughter took several years of hard knocks and destructive choices to finally settle into herself as a person. But eventually, and although the story doesn't go this way for everyone, she returned to her Christian roots and is deeply involved with her faith. While there is no way to know how her folks' consistent love and support contributed to her coming back to the God who loves her, our research shows that when kids don't feel abandoned —but instead supported—by their parents and other adults, they are more likely to develop Sticky Faith.

Growth and Change Are Necessary and Often Messy

Recently a couple approached me following a seminar I had given. They were concerned for their fourteen-year-old freshman son. He was "brilliant" but so hyper his behaviors were "off the wall." He talked back incessantly, got in minor trouble at school, and wasn't "living up to his potential."

Their question, though, related to their son's failure to respond well to their "authority" as the spiritual leaders of the household. He didn't like family devotions, he wouldn't take off his hat when they prayed, and he had stopped reading his Bible before bed. He was "lost, and we are so concerned that if we don't step in quick and hard, we'll lose him forever. What should we do?"

Obviously, there is an awful lot loaded in this brief description, and face-to-face it was even more convoluted. But let's focus on their central point: "My child is in high school, and he is changing. This change is affecting his faith. We're afraid, so what do we do?"

He Is Changing

The first thing parents must remember is that moving from childhood to adulthood can be described in a single word: change.

Change is inevitable and necessary. Your growing child will change, and change often. Sometimes you'll notice, but mostly you won't. It is as if one day you wake up to realize that who your child "is" is not the same person they were a while ago.

Generally, change means that something is happening in your child, and that is a good and important thing. Your child's movement toward maturity, exploring who he or she is, and learning how to navigate the various experiences and expectations in life will help your child settle into their own faith that lasts.

This Change Is Affecting His Faith

God created us as whole people, fully integrated, so that our perspectives and convictions all emerge from the same complex center. Generally that center is considered to be the will, the seat of our volition, where decisions are chosen and owned. This means that as your child grows, whatever they are going through in one area of life impacts all the others. As your son or daughter matures, they will begin to explore their sense of self, what they believe, and then also test out their own voice along the way. As they do, they are exhibiting growth and movement that are vital as they move into adulthood.

As parents, it is easier to celebrate the exercise of this newfound assertiveness and developing independence in some areas than in others. When your daughter arrives home and invades your small group gathering, proceeding to engage in the conversation, you swell with pride. But when that same child forcefully defends the legalization of marijuana at a dinner with extended family, you may not be so excited.

As your kids grow up, remember that they are trying to pull together a wide variety of messages, expectations, and agendas that are seeking their attention. Your investment is not minor, nor easily lost, yet your children must go through the process of deciding for themselves what path they are going to take. This process is messy and, for the short run, at least, tends to affect their faith.

We're Afraid, So What Do We Do?

I'm not sure I know any parents who do not fear, at least some, for their child and their child's future. A certain amount of parental fear is normal, keeping us on our toes, praying, looking for cues and clues to help us to respond to our kids in ways that help them as they grow. But another kind of fear—a paralyzing, crippling, breathless fear— causes us to react rather than respond, control rather than guide, force rather than shape, and dictate rather than listen. Most of us experience the former at least sometimes, but when we periodically slide into the second type of fear, that fear keeps us from being available and present for our kids. When our kids slip, our fears worsen.

When our kids falter or rebel, we need to not allow their current attitudes, behavior, or rhetoric to sway us from the course of loving and being there for them consistently. This is really our only option. Anger, overreaction, emotional battles, or desperate pleading will not be able to withstand the power of the developmental process.

What matters most is who your child is at thirty rather than what is happening at twelve or seventeen, or even twenty-two or twenty-five. Throughout adolescence your kid will try various options—lifestyles, likes and dislikes, friends, jobs, and yes, even views of God. This is what has to happen for them to become an adult. Along the way, our hope is this: parenting is a lifelong expression of nurturing tenderness and unbridled love. It is a long-term adventure, with ups and downs and wins and losses.

Whenever you are discouraged or afraid, remember that your job is not a sprint, in which every stride makes the ultimate difference. Parenting is a marathon, and pacing is what matters most.

Your Faith Impacts Your Child More Than Any Other Factor

Perhaps our most significant and summative finding regarding the influence of parents is this: how you express and live your faith will have, all things being equal, a greater impact on your child's life than any other factor. There are many other important issues that influence them as they pursue Sticky Faith. Yet what they see and hear and experience growing up with you will communicate more about the essence and veracity of faith than anything they face or anyone they know. Youth pastors, mentors, Young Life leaders, friends of faith, and other people God brings into their life may be who they talk about when they share about their faith. A special friend during high school or a unique time at camp may get the credit for sustainable Sticky Faith. But the legacy you leave will forever imprint upon your child the importance and centrality of faith.

> With my dad I definitely see a devotion to the Lord. I would walk into his room sometimes, looking for him, and walk quickly back out because he would be on his knees by his bed praying. So those images are definitely burned in my mind in terms of his commitment to the Lord and to our family.
>
> —Colette

The reality is that what matters more than looking like we are living a faithful Christian life is choosing to live a certain way because Christ has compelled us. How we interacted with a homeless person, for instance, will probably make a more indelible impression on our kids' faith than the size of the check we wrote to our church that week.

184

Sticky Faith Made Practical

When it comes to faith, we want so desperately for our kids to be strong and secure in their walk with God. We want to know that when they head off to the next stage of life, they will remain faithful and committed. But we have a dilemma: our faith can never be their faith, and yet as they are growing up, we try to force them to replicate our experience and our journey. We know we can't. But it is so hard not to, because our journey is all we know.

We end this book with our best "ideas along the journey" to help you and your kids, regardless of their life stage and spiritual path, experience the fullness of life with Christ every step along the way.

Foster a Lifelong Friendship with Your Child

The day our first child was born, he grabbed my pinky. He gurgled, squirmed, and stared into space, but he held on! He's nearly thirty, and he's had a hold on my heart every day since.

Parenthood comes with an unquenchable longing to defend, shelter, and protect. A typical parent joke is that when the first child drops her pacifier, you pick it up, run to the sink, and wash it with clean water. When the second child drops a pacifier, you pick it up, rub it on your pants, and pop it back in the kid's mouth. When the third child drops a pacifier, you ask the dog to fetch it. But joking aside, with each one, we notice, we pray, we worry, we weep.

While your kids are going through adolescence (and remember, this now includes their twenties), especially during those times of struggle or experimentation with lifestyle choices, remember that your long-term, stable commitment to be there for them regardless of what they do or how they act is your greatest gift to them. The word *respect* has morphed into something that is earned through position (as with teachers or elders) or performance. But when Peter says to deal with others with "gentleness and respect" (1 Peter 3:15), he is affirming a central tenet of God's intention for how people treat each other. You can respect your child and still disagree, even vehemently, with their choices or lifestyle. You can be their friend even when they have thoroughly disappointed you. That's the call of the gospel. That's also the lifelong call of being a parent.

When our kids shelve their faith for a time, it's so tempting to think that if we can just manipulate a few details of their situation, they'll return to their roots. This often manifests when we think, "If my daughter will just come to church with me at Christmas, she'll realize how much she needs Jesus," or "If I can just have my son and that nice young woman at church over for dinner together, my son will want to go back to church again." Of course, God can use a dinner or a church service to draw our kids back to him, but as we've learned by talking with families nationwide, that's not normally how it happens.

Restoration normally occurs through relationship. Far more important than twisting your child's arm to get them to darken the door at church is for them to know you are there for them—no matter what.

Rely on God's People for Support

Make sure you walk through life with others who will love and support you, and your son or daughter too.

We can find several sources of comfort when our kids neglect or reject faith. The most important one, of course, is God's faithfulness: the Lord loves your child far more than you do. Second, if your family has served Christ through much of your child's life, the seeds you have planted are potent and real. The evidence is clear, as we've shown in this book, that there are lots of factors that accumulate over time that can take root inside your child. The years and the rituals and prayer and conversations you have had as a family will come to your kid's mind as they move on from your direct influence. In this there can be great comfort.

But there is also the comfort of God's people. As Paul writes, "Praise be to the God and Father of our Lord Jesus Christ, the Father of compassion and the God of all comfort, who comforts us in all our troubles, so that we can comfort those in any trouble with the comfort we ourselves receive from God" (2 Cor. 1:3–4).

One of the more powerful aspects of Christian community is how God has designed us to comfort one another when we struggle. Even from those who cannot personally know what we feel, or whose experience is different from ours, we can receive the support and care we need to feel God's reassuring touch. When we open our lives to friends who share our faith and who have the ability to listen, to empathize, and especially to love and honor our kids even as they go through struggles, we receive the gift of the Holy Spirit through them.

Give Your Child to Jesus

At one point in our family's life, we were going through some dark moments. The most powerful counsel we received (and, yes, we received, or at least sat through, plenty of not-so-helpful counsel) was from a couple who had gone through parenting and come out on the other end. We knew that these friends, who were about a decade older than us, were committed to all of us and were there for us to lean on to help us navigate the circumstances.

One day they shared a particular issue that had sent them into deep questioning and anxiety over their child's choices during college. Then they described picturing Jesus standing at the top of a mountain, in all his majesty and splendor. His arms were outstretched, and his eyes were filled with compassion. He was saying, without words, "Let me take your child, for she is mine too. I love her, and I will be with her. Trust me."

This father telling me the story paused, recounting the beauty and wonder of this memory. He then looked at me and said, "I handed our daughter to Jesus. He held her, and I wept. We were so grateful and relieved. We knew the Lord was present, and real, and cared. We knew he was faithful to help her, and lift her up. Then . . ."

Pause.

"I just couldn't leave her with Jesus. I couldn't do it, even though part of me wanted to. I reached out and took her from Jesus, thanked him, and walked back down the mountain carrying our daughter, because she was our child, and we were her parents."

I could picture the scene and wanted so desperately to leave our own child with Jesus, but I knew that like the dad sharing his heart-wrenching story, I would be tempted to pick up our child and try to control the situation myself.

I was wrestling with wanting to leave our child with Jesus and wanting to step in as the parent when the father continued, "That was our journey, or actually, my journey. My wife was able to leave her there, just as she was, lying in the arms of the Savior, who loved her. But I couldn't let go. I couldn't trust him with her ... until much, much later.

"Take your child to Jesus, and leave her there."

To be honest, leaving our children with Jesus is very difficult for me. (Dee is better, but even she will admit it is very, very challenging.) I know better what it looks like when I don't leave our kids in the Lord's arms:

I pray, and weep, and journal, then drive to work fretting, bothered, and even angry;

I look for the worst in every circumstance;

I imagine the most destructive outcome of any decision or situation; and most of all,

I sneak and scheme to manipulate the circumstances that surround my kid, seeking to protect when I am actually getting in the way of their own need to learn and grow.

There are those times, however, when I find it easier, or at least more productive, to trust my child, and their life and faith journey, to Jesus Christ. In those times, I prayerfully partner with my wife, solidifying our sense that God is faithful and present. She and I spend time reflecting on the good that is present and the "wins" we see (however small), even in those times of most intense struggle.

Sometimes our children pursue ways of following Jesus that while different from our ways are nonetheless genuine and even exciting. When we see that, we encourage our child's hopes or dreams. For example, when one of our sons felt called to leave college and go to Kenya to work alongside

Masai friends, we resisted the urge to talk him out of it. Instead, we worked with him to make it possible for him to go. It was a life-changing experience for us all.

In everything we do, we seek to maintain and strengthen the trust relationship with our children, even as they are seeking their own space to find their way. This has been an important part of our parenting strategy, and it has been among our most productive. Even through the hardest of times, we have been able to keep the bond of love with each of our kids. They have told us repeatedly that this was the single most significant gift that we gave them during those times of searching.

Throughout this book, we've examined different insights from research, looked at Scripture, and culled information from a variety of valuable sources. We have offered strategies and ideas that address particular data and trends. We've shared stories from our experience with our kids and families as well as the experiences of countless parents we've met nationwide. And yet, when all is said and done, and as we've discussed in this chapter, your child's faith journey must be their own. It is ultimately between them and Jesus.

So we end this book with a simple request, one that Kara and I, and our spouses, are learning every day to live ourselves: leave your child with Jesus. Stick with Jesus always, and trust Jesus to always stick with you and your family.

sticky reflection and discussion questions

1. Think of a time when you struggled with your faith. Describe what that was like: What were the circumstances? What were some of the reasons you came back to faith in Christ?

2. Consider when you were going through the final stages of your own transition from adolescence to adulthood. What did your parents do well? What do you wish they had done differently? Where do you find yourself repeating the good, the bad, and the ugly of your parents' attitudes and actions now that you have children of your own?

3. What attitudes or behaviors might parents present or live out toward their children that could contribute to their pulling away from their parents as they attempt to make their faith their own? Now think about yourself as a parent. What attitudes or behaviors might you be showing that could possibly have the same effect on your kids?

4. What do you think your child—right now, in this place and time—needs most from you so that he or she has the best opportunity to explore faith without having to carry the burden of what you want or feel?

5. In the midst of whatever is going on with your child, what would it look like for you to leave your child with Jesus?

appendix 1

The College Transition Project Research Overview

The Fuller Youth Institute's College Transition Project is comprised of four separate research initiatives: an initial quantitative pilot study involving sixty-nine youth group graduates; two three-year longitudinal (primarily quantitative) studies of high school seniors during their first three years in college, involving 162 and 227 students respectively; and qualitative interviews with forty-five former youth group graduates between two and four years beyond high school graduation.

In 2004, the Fuller Youth Institute (FYI, at that time the Center for Youth and Family Ministry) initiated a pilot research study called the College Transition Project (CTP), surveying a group of sixty-nine college students who were alumni of a single youth group in the Northwest. The preliminary results suggested a link between a college student's current spiritual state and the quality of key relationships during the high school years, including the youth group environment itself. As a result, in 2005–06 FYI launched a broader study, recruiting students involved in church youth groups during the spring of their high school senior year. To participate in the survey, students were required to be over eighteen years of age, be part of a church youth group, and intend to attend a college or university upon graduation. Students were recruited through FYI's nationwide network of youth leader contacts, resulting in a sample of 162 students who were surveyed four times over three years. Thirty of these students participated in subsequent one-hour interviews during their fourth year out of high school.

In 2006–07, made possible by funding from the Lilly Endowment, FYI launched another nationwide longitudinal study of high school seniors connected to church youth groups to examine their experiences at five points: the spring of their senior year in high school (2007), the fall and spring of their first year in college (2007 and 2008), the spring of their second year in college (2009), and the spring of their third year in college (2010). The primary goal of the study was to determine whether there are programmatic and relational characteristics of high school youth ministries and churches that have a demonstrable relationship to how students make the faith adjustment to life beyond high school.

Participants

The sample for this longitudinal study launched in 2007 consisted of 227 high school seniors drawn from different regions across the United States. More than half (56.3%) of the respondents were female while 43.7% were male. The sample was predominantly white/Caucasian (78.0%). Asian/Asian American students comprised 11.0 percent of the sample, while Hispanic/Latino students accounted for 5.0

percent. African-American and Native American students each accounted for 1.4 percent of the sample. Participants reported a median grade point average of 3.5 to 3.99, with 63 percent of the sample having GPAs above 3.5. Given that 88 percent of seniors who apply to college have a GPA over 3.0, our sample represents a high-achieving group.[1] The majority of the participants came from larger churches. The median youth group size was 51 to 100 students, while the median church size was reported to be over 800 members.

Participants were mostly from intact families, with 83.8 percent reporting that they lived with both their father and mother; another 4.1 percent lived with a parent and steppar-ent. Overall, the parents of the participants were well edu-cated. More than two-thirds (69.7%) of the mothers held at least a college degree; this figure was nearly three-quarters for the fathers (73.0%). By far the majority of the fathers (88.2%) of the participants were employed full-time, while fewer than half of the mothers were (42.5%).

Procedure

From October 2006 to February 2007, members of the research team who had developed networks in four geo-graphical regions of the United States (the Southwest, the Northwest, the Southeast, and the Northeast) identified churches representing size, denominational, socioeconomic, and ethnic diversity. For this study, only churches employing full-time youth pastors were recruited. From March to June 2007, the youth ministry staff of each participating church was asked to invite senior students involved in their youth ministries to participate in the study. As with the previous study, students were eligible only if they were eighteen years old or over and intended to attend a college upon graduation.

Students who agreed to participate in the study could do so in one of three ways: they could complete a paper-and-pencil version of the survey together (facilitated either by their youth pastor or a member of the FYI research team), they could complete a paper version of the survey individually at a time and place convenient to them, or they could complete an online version of the survey. In addition to the survey, each student was required to complete a consent form assuring confidentiality. Signed consent forms also contained an identification code that was unique to each individual, as well as contact information (i.e., an email address and a physical address) in order to track each student for future waves of data collection. All future data collection was done via online surveys.

Instruments

Faith Measures

Five measures of faith development were employed to create a composite picture of both internalized and externalized faith commitments and behaviors. For four of the measures, participants were asked to rate their agreement on a five-point scale, ranging from *strongly disagree* (1) to *strongly agree* (5). The Intrinsic Religious Motivation Scale[2] is comprised of ten items measuring the extent to which an individual's religiosity is not simply external and behavioral but internalized in terms of one's values and motivations. Sample items include "My faith involves all of my life" and "I try hard to carry my religion over into all my other dealings in life." A similar measure, the Narrative Faith Relevance Scale,[3] assesses the extent to which one's decisions are influenced by the sense of having a relationship with God. Sample items include "If and when I date someone, it is (or would be) important to me that God be pleased with the relationship" and "In choosing what college to attend, it was important to me to seek God's will." The third measure is the seventeen-item short form of the Search Institute's Faith Maturity Scale,[4] including items like "My faith shapes how I think and act each and every day" and "My life is committed to Jesus Christ." And the fourth is the Religious Support Scale,[5] assessing the extent to which participants feel supported and nurtured by God. Using social support items, the scale incorporates indicators such as "I am valued by God."

The fifth measure is a measure of religious behavior created for the CTP pilot. Ten items assess the frequency of engagement in a variety of corporate and individual behaviors, including such items as "pray alone," "read the Bible by yourself," and "attend a worship service or church-related event with your parents." Responses are given on a six-point scale, ranging from *less than once a month* (1) to *once a day or more* (6).

Youth Group Experience Measures

Three sets of items were created from qualitative data from earlier stages of the project in order to assess students' participation in and attitudes toward their youth group experience. First, students were asked about the frequency of participation over the past two months or the past year in eight items, including activities like retreats, mission trips, and midweek youth group. Second, participants were presented with twenty-two statements representing why students go to youth group, including "It's where my friends are" and "I learn about God there." Students were asked to rate how true each statement was for them using a five-point scale ranging from *not true at all* (1) to *completely true* (5). Third, students were asked what they would want to see more or less of in their youth group. Thirteen items were presented, such as "one-on-one time with leaders" and "mission trips." Participants responded on a five-point scale ranging from *much less* (1) to *much more* (5).

Other Measures

In addition to these faith and youth ministry measures, other scales and questions were added related to perceived social support, parental support, support within the youth ministry, loneliness, extraversion, social desirability (as a control factor), and risk behaviors (sexual contact, alcohol use, and pornography use). Subsequent waves of data collection have included most of these same measures (particularly faith measures), in addition to scales and questions related to religious behaviors in college, the college spiritual environment, adjustment to college, doubts about faith, parental and other adult contact in college, parental faith discussions, preparation for decision making, and college participation in church and campus ministry.

The following are some of the spirituality instruments and their corresponding items.

Intrinsic Religious Motivation Scale

1. My faith involves all of my life.
2. One should seek God's guidance when making every important decision.
3. It doesn't matter so much what I believe as long as I live a moral life.
4. In my life, I experience the presence of the Divine.
5. My faith sometimes restricts my actions.
6. Although I am a religious person, I refuse to let religious considerations influence my everyday affairs.
7. Nothing is as important to me as serving God as best I know how.
8. Although I believe in my religion, I feel there are many more important things in life.
9. I try hard to carry my religion over into all my other dealings in life.
10. My religious beliefs are what really lie behind my whole approach to life.[6]

Narrative Faith Relevance Scale

1. It is important to me that my future career somehow embody a calling from God.
2. I try to see setbacks and crises as part of God's larger plan.
3. If and when I date someone, it is (or would be) important to me that God be pleased with the relationship.
4. In thinking about my schedule, I try to cultivate the attitude that my time belongs to God.

5. It is important to me that whatever money I have be used to serve God's purposes.

6. In choosing what college to attend, it is important to me to seek God's will.

7. When I think of the things I own or would like to own, I try to remember that everything I have belongs to God.[7]

Faith Maturity Scale

1. I experience a deep communion with God.

2. My faith shapes how I think and act each and every day.

3. I help others with their religious questions and struggles.

4. My faith helps me know right from wrong.

5. I devote time to reading and studying the Bible.

6. Every day I see evidence that God is active in the world.

7. I seek out opportunities to help me grow spiritually.

8. I take time for periods of prayer or meditation.

9. I feel God's presence in my relationships with other people.

10. My life is filled with meaning and purpose.

11. I try to apply my faith to political and social issues.

12. My life is committed to Jesus Christ.

13. I go out of my way to show love to people I meet.

14. I have a real sense that God is guiding me.

15. I like to worship and pray with others.

16. I think Christians must be about the business of creating international understanding and harmony.

17. I am spiritually moved by the beauty of God's creation.[8]

Religious Support Scale

1. God gives me the sense that I belong.

2. I feel appreciated by God.

3. If something went wrong, God would give me help.

4. I am valued by God.

5. I can turn to God for advice when I have problems.

6. God cares about my life and situation.

7. I do *not* feel close to God.[9]

High School Version of Religious Behavior Scale
(Created for the CTP Pilot Project)

For the following eight items, please tell us how often you engaged in each of the behaviors listed, during *the past twelve months*: Less than once a month, About once a month, Two to three times a month, About once a week, Two to three times a week, Daily.

How often did you:

1. talk with another Christian about your faith, outside of a church-related context?

2. pray alone?

3. attend a worship service or church-related event?

4. speak or try to speak with a non-Christian about your faith?

5. volunteer your time to serve others?

6. participate in a small group of your peers for religious or spiritual purposes?

7. read your Bible by yourself?

8. meet with a spiritual mentor (other than your parents)?

College Version of Religious Behavior Scale

How often did you:

1. talk with another Christian about your faith, outside of a church-related context?
2. participate in an on-campus Christian fellowship?
3. pray alone?
4. attend a worship service or other event at a church off-campus?
5. speak or try to speak with a non-Christian about your faith?
6. volunteer your time to serve others?
7. participate in a small group of your peers for religious or spiritual purposes?
8. read your Bible by yourself?
9. attend a school-sponsored chapel?
10. meet with an older Christian for spiritual growth, mentoring, or discipleship?
11. participate in service or justice work that helps people in need?

appendix 2

The Hurt Project
Research Overview

An Ongoing Research Project;
Chap Clark, PhD, Lead Researcher

The Hurt Project research, used as a significant contributor to this book, is driven by the data, results, conclusions, discussions, and limitations of an initial two-part study conducted by a research team and me from 2001 to early 2004, as well as the added data from the third phase (2004–10). The initial phase of the project was driven by the data discovered in my role as a substitute teacher from late 2001 to June 2002 at Crescenta Valley High School in the Glendale Unified School District using an ethnographic methodology known as participant observation. At the same time, our team conducted a thorough literature review of all relevant material, both popular and academic sources, that served to inform, shape, and nuance these observations and emerging perspectives. The second phase of the project, from the summer of 2002 to spring 2004, consisted of seventeen open-ended conversations with high school juniors and seniors in which I sought to gather a new batch of data giving texture and thickness to the observations and literature reviews previously utilized. This is what was reported in the first edition of the book *Hurt: Inside the World of Today's Teenagers*. The continuing phase of the project is an ongoing synthesis of observation, interviews, open-ended conversations, and deliberate focus groups that provide additional data to the original results, pushing against conclusions that have changed or at least slightly morphed over the past several years, and more specifically focusing on populations and environments that the original study understudied.

While participant observation was the initial and motivating strategy used for the study, each supporting methodology we used was integrated in such a way as to bring out the most complete and robust picture of teenagers' sense of their world and life. While there are a myriad of possible ways to investigate the general sense of adolescents' perception of their reality, what is vital is that any methodology must be able to provide a relatively authentic and honest portrait of those being studied. As Paula Saukko notes, "The worth or validity of [a] project depends on how thoroughly and defensibly or correctly [it] has been done."[1]

The data reported is the integration of a four-part research process: my role as participant observer in a high school, a literature review team investigating the issues that emerged from my observation, a series of conversations and focus groups, and an ongoing synthesis of observations, conversations, and focus groups, interaction with new scholarship, and a proactive commitment to dialogue with practitioners and scholars.

Participant Observation/Ethnography

Perhaps the most fundamental question a social scientist can ask is, "How do we really *know* about a given population?" As the lead researcher in the Hurt Project, I have wrestled long and hard with this question for nearly a decade. As the world changes and widespread cultural trends increasingly demonstrate how these changes affect us all, this question is increasingly prompting scholars, albeit somewhat reluctantly for many, to move in a little closer to those who can teach the most about their world, in this case the adolescents themselves. Today's teenagers have a great deal more to share than what we can often see and know through the more typical focus groups, questionnaires, or even personal interviews. Especially when studying adolescents, answers do not always remain consistent, and sometimes actual, on-the-street, lived-out beliefs and perspectives do not correlate with what they might say to a researcher.

To even begin to paint an accurate picture of the complex, multitiered world of today's teenager, it takes someone who is outside of the constantly changing nature of adolescence to carefully listen, watch, ask, invite, and pursue.[2] It takes someone who is close enough to get a well-rounded picture of what is going on but at the same time is considered safe enough to invite authentic and unfiltered behaviors and conversation. Patricia and Peter Adler, leading ethnographic scholars, affirm that participant observation is a most productive methodology for studying adolescent life and behavior, as they describe in the *Journal of Contemporary Ethnography*: "Given ethnography's strength of getting inside groups' innerworkings, this methodology has been central to the exploration of how teenagers make sense of their social worlds."[3]

The specific strategy I employed was to find a way to honor the agreement with the school and district to serve as a substitute teacher, while at the same time observing the students. I maintained the integrity of the role by following the directions the teacher had left regarding the class, and the co-principals and I agreed that the students (and faculty and administrators) should also be made aware of why I was there beyond substitute teaching. I would begin every class by explaining that I was on a lengthy sabbatical leave in order to listen to and observe the world of high school students and that I was planning to write a book about what I saw and heard. At the end of each day, I would record impressions — without using any names of students or even specific classes — of what I observed that day. At the end of each week I would synthesize my diary notes into a loose but comprehensive narrative, and then put the daily logs away. Within a few weeks, themes began to emerge, and I would allow myself to reflectively test out these emerging themes in my future daily observations.

During the semester-plus I was on campus, I received over a thousand unsolicited poems, notes, songs, and letters from students (and a few teachers). Later our team coded these texts (changing the names of students) and my observations, conversations, and preliminary conclusions to create a database. Kathy Charmaz suggests this type of data coding is an important aspect of the participant observer's process in order to allow for various random materials to be integrated and synthesized. She writes, "Coding gives a researcher analytic scaffolding on which to build. Because researchers study their empirical materials closely, they can define both new leads from them and gaps in them. Each piece of data—whether an interview, a field note, a case study, a personal account, or a document—can inform earlier data."[4]

Literature Review

While the Hurt Project initially relied on my work on a high school campus, we have also taken great care to align, or at least measure, our conclusions with relevant literature. Our commitment to a thorough interdisciplinary literature review, then, provides as much of a dynamic data set as any of the other forms of data collection we used. In participant observation, the literature review offers a grounding and boundarying structure that enables open-ended ethnographic inquiry while at the same time a place for contextualized analysis. The literature review is vital because it forces an ethnographic researcher to either position observations and conclusions within a previously delineated conceptual framework or, if necessary, push for a new way of thinking. This is what maintains ethnography in general and participant observation in particular as a bona fide and trustworthy social science methodology.[5]

In participant observation, the conceptual boundaries that literature provides, however, must not be allowed to shape ideas and perspectives before the observations themselves have bubbled to the surface of the researcher's impressions. In other words, relevant literature should be used as a potential corrective to observations and conclusions that violate previous theoretical assumptions, not to *a priori* shape the impressions. Throughout both the initial study and the ongoing work of the Hurt study, that is how we have employed relevant literature and theory.

Informal Conversations and Focus Groups

Focus groups and their research cousins, informal group conversations, have been shown to provide ethnographers with a wealth of insight not easily captured using other methods. First, even the most astute participant observer is able to see only snapshots of a given population, so a focus group will be able to fill in gaps.[6] In addition, focus groups can help researchers avoid forming premature conclusions before having enough firsthand information.[7] I found our procedure of adjusting conclusions according to the focus group comments to be vital to our overall understanding of this population. And last, the greatest value of the focus groups was the way the teenagers were able to "reveal unarticulated norms and normative assumptions"[8] that in many cases I generally suspected but were made clear by the collective descriptive and corporate assent of the group participants. Thus throughout the entire project and since, we have utilized some form of small group interaction as a third primary source of data.

The groups were comprised of fifteen to twenty high school juniors and seniors and were chosen from at least three, and usually six to ten, population pools that were all geographically proximate.[9] The cities and communities were chosen to represent a wide spectrum of US population centers and to represent a wide demographic as well—ethnic, urban, rural, suburban, and so on. (I also conducted two Canadian focus groups, one each on the east and west coast.) Before arriving in a city or town, I contacted at least two local nongovernmental agencies (and usually more) to enlist their help with contacting youth and youth-serving organizations to find potential subjects who were "articulate and willing to discuss with peers, many of whom they would not know, their impressions of the world they lived in, for a research project seeking to understand how teenagers perceive their life and world." Each city ended up with a unique process, but our team was insistent on the following conditions: if at all possible, no more than three of the students would know each other well, no more than 50 percent could be actively involved in any single major category (sports team, church and/or religious youth organization, service club, etc.), the participants had to be available for a one-time sitting (including pizza), and a parent had to sign a release form. In most cases we followed up with a letter to each parent asking to reaffirm their willingness for their child to participate. In the years since the first edition, I have conducted between eight and fifteen similar conversations, with varying levels of formality.

The format of the groups was straightforward. We wanted to allow for perspectives to emerge without being shaped by the presence of the researcher or the way a question was asked. Therefore I came alone to almost every focus group and took notes sparingly, trying to stay true to the observation method by relying on my memory, except for direct or especially pithy quotes. In deciding how to facilitate the groups, we chose to err on the side of simplicity and openness by making statements like "Tell me about school" or "Discuss friends" (or dating or family or pressure). Once the teens achieved a level of safety with each other, usually within the first thirty to forty-five minutes, the most important work I had to do was to avoid group-think, times when the discussion appeared to be swelling into too clean of a uniformity. The research on how facilitators can avoid groupthink is well documented, and prevention of groupthink is a relatively easily accessed skill set, employing strategies like inviting a quiet person to answer a relatively unrelated question, or by reintroducing or redirecting words one subject has used that would contradict the direction the group was headed.[10] This proved not to be a problem with any of the groups.

The Ongoing Work of the Hurt Project

As stated, the work of the Hurt Project was not complete with the release of the book. As a graduate school professor, I have continued to enlist students and graduates to investigate a wide range of literature, to ask ethnographic questions while in the field, and to personally work with and consult organizations and communities that seek to do a better job understanding and serving teenagers. Our teams have chosen to see this research as an ongoing inquiry and to report what is seen and heard in the natural course of networks and relationships, as opposed to formalizing the project by means of a committee, grant, or institutional project. Instead, for example, when a private school invites me (or a member of my team) to spend time on their campus observing and interviewing students and faculty to determine the level and places of systemic abandonment, we operate under the guidelines of the institution and authority of their board of directors. When given the opportunity to conduct focus groups, we do insist, as we have from the beginning, on parental consent, but for the most part we observe and operate under the auspices of the inviting party.

Finally, the reason we have continued this project, and will continue this project for years to come, is that what was discovered in writing the original book *Hurt* is not improving. The level of responsibility and competencies[11] required of children from very early ages has risen exponentially over the past decade, and yet the ongoing adult support and guidance offered to them without a self-serving agenda has diminished at roughly the same rate. We are convinced that children and teenagers have never experienced less social capital than they do today and that they experience more stress than any generation in history. We stand with a growing group of people who are committed to raising the flag of awareness, conversation, and action so that our children, and their children, will grow up in a world where they are known, loved, and cherished.

notes

chapter 1: the not-so-sticky-faith reality

1. Laurie Goodstein, "Evangelicals Fear the Loss of Their Teenagers," *New York Times*, October 6, 2006.

2. For example, in September 2006, the Barna Group released their observation that "the most potent data regarding disengagement is that a majority of twentysomethings—61 percent of today's young adults— had been churched at one point during their teen years but they are now spiritually disengaged" (Barna Group, "Most Twentysomethings Put Christianity on the Shelf Following Spiritually Active Teen Years," *Barna Update*, September 16, 2006). According to Gallup polls, approximately 40 percent of eighteen- to twenty-nine-year-olds who attended church when they were sixteen or seventeen years old are no longer attending (George H. Gallup Jr., "The Religiosity Cycle," *The Gallup Poll*, October 19, 2006; Frank Newport, "A Look at Religious Switching in America Today," *The Gallup Poll*, October 19, 2006).

A 2007 survey by LifeWay Research of over a thousand adults ages eighteen to thirty who spent a year or more in youth group during high school suggests that more than 65 percent of young adults who attend a Protestant church for at least a year in high school will stop attending church regularly for at least a year between the ages of eighteen and twenty-two (LifeWay, "LifeWay Research Uncovers Reasons 18 to 22 Year Olds Drop Out of Church," LifeWay Christian Resources, *http:// www.lifeway.com/article/165949/*). In this study, respondents were not necessarily people who had graduated from youth group as seniors. In addition, the research design did not factor in parachurch or on-campus faith communities in their definition of college church attendance.

Data from the National Study of Youth and Religion published in 2009 indicate an approximate 30 percent drop in weekly or more often religious service attendance across multiple Protestant denominations (Christian Smith and Patricia Snell, *Souls in Transition: The Religious and Spiritual Lives of Emerging Adults* [New York: Oxford University Press, 2009]).

Fuller Youth Institute's estimate that 40 to 50 percent of high school graduates will fail to stick with their faith is based on a compilation of data from these various studies.

3. Quite a while after we started using the term *Sticky Faith* in our writing and seminars, we learned that there was a book by Group Publishing entitled *Sticky Faith*. A year later, we read the phrase "sticky faith" in Diana Garland's *Inside Out Families*. While we came up with the term *Sticky Faith* independently, we are glad that other thoughtful leaders are devoting energy to helping kids' and families' faith stick.

4. LifeWay, "LifeWay Research Uncovers Reasons."

5. The percentage varies greatly by denomination; conservative Protestants are more likely to return than Roman Catholics or mainline Protestants (Wade Clark Roof and Lyn Gesch, "Boomers and the Culture of Choice: Changing Patterns of Work, Family, and Religion," in *Work, Family, and Religion in Contemporary Society*, ed. Nancy Tatom Ammerman and Wade Clark Roof [New York: Routledge, 1995], 61–79).

6. The National Center on Addiction and Substance Abuse at Columbia University, "Wasting the Best and the Brightest: Substance Abuse at America's Colleges and Universities," *http://www.casacolumbia.org/download.aspx?path=/UploadedFiles/b1kms01k.pdf*.

7. Henry Wechsler and Bernice Wuetrich, *Dying to Drink: Confronting Binge Drinking on College Campuses* (Emmaus, Penn.: Rodale, 2002), 4, 21.

8. Ibid., 4, 28.

9. Michael Kimmel, *Guyland* (New York: HarperCollins, 2008), 199.

10. Ibid., 195.

11. Ibid., 58.

12. Carolyn McNamara Barry and Larry J. Nelson, "The Role of Religion in the Transition to Adulthood for Young Emerging Adults," *Journal of Youth and Adolescence* 34, no. 3 (2005): 245–55; Patrick L. Dulin, Robert D. Hill, and Kari Ellingson, "Relationships among Religious Factors, Social Support and Alcohol Abuse in a Western U.S. College Student Sample," *Journal of Alcohol and Drug Education* 50, no. 1 (2004): 5–14;

Eva S. Lefkowitz, Meghan M. Gillen, Cindy L. Shearer, and Tanya L. Boone, "Religiosity, Sexual Behaviors, and Sexual Attitudes during Emerging Adulthood," *Journal of Sex Research* 41, no. 2 (2004): 150–59; Melissa S. Strawser, Eric A. Storch, Gary R. Geffken, Erin M. Killiany, and Audrey L. Baumeister, "Religious Faith and Substance Problems in Undergraduate College Students: A Replication," *Pastoral Psychology* 53, no. 2 (2004): 183–88.

13. Chap Clark, *Hurt: Inside the World of Today's Teenagers* (Grand Rapids, Mich.: Baker Academic, 2004), now in a completely revised and updated version, *Hurt 2.0*, released June 2011.

14. Thanks to a sizable research grant from the Lilly Endowment, central to our College Transition Project are two longitudinal studies of 384 youth group seniors through their first three years in college. We designed our College Transition Project research to be longitudinal, meaning we followed youth group graduates over time, so that we could track their individual and collective journeys during their first three years in college. The majority of the students we surveyed took their first online questionnaire during the spring of their senior year in high school, then one or two online questionnaires per year during their freshman, sopho-more, and junior years in college. Each wave of data collection allowed us to peel away less significant layers of the transition and focus on what lay at the Sticky Faith core. Please note our research was not designed to prove causation but to discover strong correlations between variables that might predict the relationships between those variables.

15. The College Transition Project is comprised of four separate research initiatives: an initial quantitative pilot study involving sixty-nine youth group graduates, two three-year longitudinal (primarily quantitative) studies of high school seniors during their first three years in college, involving 162 and 227 students respectively, and additional qualitative interviews with forty-five former youth group graduates who are currently in college. For more on our research methodology, visit *www.stickyfaith.org*.

16. LifeWay, "LifeWay Research Uncovers Reasons."

17. We wrestled with how to describe the fact that God cares about and interacts with each individual and yet much of our faith growth is communal. *Personal* is our best attempt, but in using that term, we do not mean to imply an individualistic faith.

18. Based on these three descriptors, we quantified Sticky Faith through a compilation of valid and reliable faith maturity scales that focus on internalized paradigms and beliefs, motivation for those values and beliefs, and more externalized behaviors (both public and private faith practices like prayer, service, and church attendance).

19. Christian Smith with Melinda Lundquist Denton, *Soul Searching: The Religious and Spiritual Lives of American Teenagers* (New York: Oxford Univ. Press, 2005), 56.

20. Listen to the "Soul Searching" panel discussion from March 2008 at the FYI website: *http://fulleryouthinstitute.org/2008/03/soul -searching-panel/.*

21. Tim Clydesdale, *The First Year Out* (Chicago: Univ. of Chicago Press, 2007), 205.

chapter 2: the sticky gospel

1. Dallas Willard, *The Divine Conspiracy* (New York: HarperCollins, 1998), 41.

2. "Command them to do good, to be rich in good deeds, and to be generous and willing to share" (1 Tim. 6:18).

chapter 3: sticky identity

1. For this book we have chosen to use the labels of child (birth – 10), early adolescent (10 – 14), late adolescent (14 – 18/20), emerging adult (a term offered by Jeffrey J. Arnett for ages 18/20 – late 20s), and adult (late 20s and beyond).

2. A comprehensive website for more information on the adolescent brain is from the Society for Neuroscience: Advancing the Understanding of the Brain and Nervous System at *http://www.sfn.org/index .aspx?pagename=brainBriefings_Adolescent_brain* (accessed May 2, 2011).

3. While there is ample evidence that this is observably true, scholars have yet to agree on specific causes or even impact. There is no doubt, however, that there is a massive social shift occurring where we now have four stages of development instead of three: child, adolescent, emerging adult, and adult (see Jeffery J. Arnett, *Adolescence and Emerging Adulthood: A Cultural Approach* [Upper Saddle River, N.J.: Pearson Edu-

cation, 2000]). For more on this, we suggest three books that provide a fairly uniform summary of the issue but offer different causes and solutions: Chap Clark, *Hurt 2.0: Inside the World of Today's Teenagers*, 2nd ed. (Grand Rapids, Mich.: Baker Academic, 2011); Robert Epstein, *Teen 2.0* (Fresno, Calif.: Linden Publishing, 2010); and Christian Smith and Patricia Snell, *Souls in Transition: The Religious and Spiritual Lives of Emerging Adults* (New York: Oxford Univ. Press, 2009).

4. See Tim Clydesdale, *The First Year Out* (Chicago: Univ. of Chicago Press, 2007).

5. Thanks to Dr. Cheryl Crawford of Azusa Pacific University for her contributions to this section.

6. The foundational Nouwen books explaining these thoughts are *In the Name of Jesus* and *Life of the Beloved*.

7. Thanks to author and friend Philip Yancey for this expression that has become almost a cliché in our family.

8. Robert Kegan, *In over Our Heads: The Mental Demands of Modern Life* (Cambridge, Mass.: Harvard Univ. Press, 1994), 42.

chapter 4: sticky faith conversations

1. Search Institute, *Effective Christian Education: A National Study of Protestant Congregations* (Minneapolis: Search Institute, 1990).

2. These two data sets are the National Study of Youth and Religion and the National Longitudinal Study of Adolescent Health (Mark D. Regnerus, *Forbidden Fruit* [New York: Oxford Univ. Press, 2007], 60–73).

3. This finding emerged from questions related to the degree of freedom kids feel to discuss their doubts in their youth ministry. Our guess is that the same dynamic holds for discussions about doubt in the family.

4. Dallas Willard, *The Divine Conspiracy* (San Francisco: HarperSanFrancisco, 1998), 40.

5. Derek Melleby, "Life after High School: The First Year," Center for Parent/Youth Understanding, *http://www.cpyu.org/Page.aspx?id=387650*.

chapter 5: a sticky web of relationships

1. Judith Gundry-Volf, "To Such as These Belongs the Reign of God," *Theology Today* 56, no. 4 (2000): 475–76.

2. Sharon Daloz Parks, *Big Questions, Worthy Dreams* (San Francisco: Jossey-Bass, 2000), 192.

3. Erika C. Knuth, "Intergenerational Connections and Faith Development in Late Adolescence" (PhD diss., Fuller Theological Seminary Graduate School of Psychology, 2010).

4. Reggie Joiner, Chuck Bomar, and Abbie Smith, *The Slow Fade* (Colorado Springs: Cook, 2010), 63.

5. Reggie Joiner and Carey Nieuwhof, *Parenting beyond Your Capacity* (Colorado Springs: Cook, 2010), 70.

6. David Fraze, "A Church in the Intergenerational HOV Lane," *FYI E-Journal*, February 2, 2009, *http://fulleryouthinstitute.org/2009/02/a-church-in-the-intergenerational-hov-lane/*.

7. Stanley Hauerwas, Carole Bailey Stokeking, Keith G. Meador, and David Cloutier, *Growing Old in Christ* (Grand Rapids, Mich.: Eerdmans, 2003), 182.

chapter 6: sticky justice

1. Nicholas Wolterstorff, "The Contours of Justice: An Ancient Call for Shalom," in *God and the Victim: Theological Reflections on Evil, Victimization, Justice, and Forgiveness*, ed. Lisa Barnes Lampman and Michelle D. Shattuck (Grand Rapids, Mich.: Eerdmans, 1999), 113.

2. Tim Arango, "Make Room, Cynics; MTV Wants to Do Some Good," *New York Times*, April 18, 2009, *http://www.nytimes.com/2009/04/19/business/media/19mtv.html?th&emc=th*.

3. David A. Livermore, *Cultural Intelligence: Improving Your CQ to Engage Our Multicultural World* (Grand Rapids, Mich.: Baker Academic, 2009), 26.

4. Kurt Ver Beek, "The Impact of Short-Term Missions: A Case Study of House Construction in Honduras after Hurricane Mitch," *Missiology* 34, no. 4 (October 2006): 485.

5. Robert J. Priest, Terry Dischinger, Steve Rasmussen, and C. M. Brown, "Researching the Short-Term Mission Movement," *Missiology* 34, no. 4, (October 2006): 431–50.

6. MTV's national survey was comprised of 1,308 twelve- to twenty-four-year-olds who completed online surveys and ninety-eight students who were interviewed personally.

7. This research can be accessed at *http://www.mtv.com/thinkmtv/ research/*.

8. Sara Corbett, "A Prom Divided," *New York Times*, May 21, 2009, *http://www.nytimes.com/2009/05/24/magazine/24prom-t.html*.

9. Diana Garland, *Inside Out Families* (Waco, Tex.: Baylor Univ. Press, 2010), 70.

10. We are deeply indebted to our coresearchers, Dave Livermore and Terry Linhart, for the design and facilitation of these summits, in addition to all of the participants who sacrificially gave their time and deep insights: Jared Ayers, George Bache, Noel Becchetti, Terry Bley, Todd Bratulich, Tom Carpenter, Sean Cooper, April Diaz, Brian Dietz, Joel Fay, Hal Hamilton, Brian Heerwagen, Eric Iverson, Tom Ives, Cari Jenkins, Johnny Johnston, Kent Koteskey, Sandy Liu, Mark Maines, Mark Matlock, Daryl Nuss, Derry Prenkert, Kurt Rietema, David Russell, David Schultz, Rich Van Pelt, Bob Whittet, and Kimberly Williams.

11. The following section is adapted from Kara Powell, Dave Livermore, Terry Linhart, and Brad Griffin, "If We Send Them, They Will Grow ... Maybe," *http://fulleryouthinstitute.org/2007/03/if-we-send-them-they -will-grow%E2%80%A6maybe/*.

12. Laura Joplin, "On Defining Experiential Education," in *The Theory of Experiential Education*, ed. Karen Warren, Mitchell Sakofs, and Jasper S. Hunt Jr. (Dubuque, Ia.: Kendall/Hunt, 1995), 15–22.

13. Terrence D. Linhart, "Planting Seeds: The Curricular Hope of Short Term Mission Experiences in Youth Ministry," *Christian Education Journal*, 3rd ser. (2005): 256–72. Some of the terminology in the model has been modified.

14. This model is fully explained in Kara Powell and Brad Griffin, *Deep Justice Journeys* (Grand Rapids, Mich.: Zondervan, 2009). In *Deep Justice Journeys*, fifty before/during/after learning activities are provided to help teenagers move from mission trips to missional living.

15. Garland, *Inside Out Families*, 116.

chapter 7: a sticky bridge out of home

1. The seminal work on this theory of a liminal period can be found in Arnold Van Gennep, *The Rites of Passage*, trans. Monika B. Vizedom and Garielle L. Caffee (1908; Chicago: Univ. of Chicago Press, 1960), and

Victor Turner and Edith Turner, *Image and Pilgrimage in Christian Culture: Anthropological Perspectives* (New York: Columbia Univ. Press, 1978).

2. I am grateful to FYI's associate director, Brad Griffin, for his collaboration on this chapter.

3. Tim Clydesdale, *The First Year Out* (Chicago: Univ. of Chicago Press, 2007), 2, also see 73–74.

4. According to Kathy Chu, "College Students Using Plastic More," *USA Today*, April 13, 2009, and "Credit Card Statistics, Industry Facts, Debt Statistics," *http://www.creditcards.com/credit-card-news/credit-card -industry-facts-personal-debt-statistics-1276.php* (accessed March 2, 2011).

5. Kenneth R. Mitchell and Herbert Anderson, *All Our Losses, All Our Griefs: Resources for Pastoral Care* (Louisville: Westminster, 1983), 36–46.

Appendix 1: The College Transition Project Research Overview

1. Xianglei Chen, Joanna Wu, Shayna Tasoff, "The High School Senior Class of 2003–04: Steps toward Postsecondary Enrollment," US Department of Education, National Center for Education Statistics, February 2010, table 4, *http://nces.ed.gov/pubs2010/2010203.pdf*.

2. D. R. Hoge, "A Validated Intrinsic Religious Motivation Scale," *Journal for the Scientific Study of Religion* 11 (1972): 369–76.

3. Cameron Lee, "Narrative Faith Relevance Scale" (unpublished manuscript, 2004).

4. P. L. Benson, M. J. Donahue, and J. A. Erickson, "The Faith Maturity Scale: Conceptualization, Measurement, and Empirical Validation," *Research in the Social Scientific Study of Religion* 5 (1993): 1–26.

5. William E. Fiala, Jeffrey P. Bjorck, and Richard Gorsuch, "The Religious Support Scale: Construction, Validation, and Cross-Validation," *American Journal of Community Psychology* 30 (2002): 761–86.

6. Hoge, "Validated Intrinsic Religious Motivation Scale."

7. Lee, "Narrative Faith Relevance Scale."

8. Benson et al., "The Faith Maturity Scale."

9. Fiala et al., "The Religious Support Scale."

Appendix 2: The Hurt Project

1. Paula Saukko, "Methodologies for Cultural Studies: An Integrative Approach," in *The SAGE Handbook of Qualitative Research*, 3rd ed., ed. Norman K. Denzin and Yvonna S. Lincoln (Thousand Oaks, Calif.: SAGE, 2005), 346.

2. An example of this is Michelle Fine and Lois Weis's report on injustice toward American high school youth. Through their ethnographic, close-up investigation, they were able to see that "unlike most students in U.S. schools, youth in desegregated schools must theorize their own identities relationally all the time and every day, because they are making selves in spaces where 'difference' matters. That is, they are learning, claiming, and negotiating their places in a microcosmic racial/classed hierarchy on a daily basis." This level of observation could not have come solely from the more typical forms of studying teenagers, like a survey. There is too much direct insight and too intimate a familiarity with the circumstances of those being studied to have been discovered without some form and level of participant observation. Michelle Fine and Lois Weis, "Compositional Studies, in Two Parts: Critical Theorizing and Analysis on Social (In)Justice," in Denzin and Lincoln, *SAGE Handbook of Qualitative Research*, 75.

3. Patricia A. Adler and Peter Adler, "Review Essay: Teen Scenes: Ethnographies of Adolescent Cultures," *Journal of Contemporary Ethnography* 31 (October 2002): 653.

4. Kathy Charmaz, "Grounded Theory in the 21st Century: Applications for Advancing Social Justice Studies," in Denzin and Lincoln, *SAGE Handbook of Qualitative Research*, 517.

5. "Ethnography's 'self-correcting investigative process' has typically included adequate and appropriate sampling procedures, systematic techniques for gathering and analyzing data, validation of data, avoidance of observer bias, and documentation of findings" (Michael V. Angrosino, "Reconstructing Observation: Ethnography, Pedagogy, and the Prospects for a Progressive Political Agenda, in Denzin and Lincoln, *SAGE Handbook of Qualitative Research*, 733).

6. George Kamberelis and Greg Dimitriadis, "Focus Groups: Strategic Articulations of Pedagogy, Politics, and Inquiry," in Denzin and Lincoln, *SAGE Handbook of Qualitative Research*, 887–907.

7. As George Kamberelis and Greg Dimitriadis note, "And perhaps most important, the dialogic possibilities afforded by focus groups help researchers to work against premature consolidation of their understandings and explanations, thereby signaling the limits of reflexivity and the importance of intellectual/empirical modesty as forms of ethics and praxis. Such modesty allows us to engage in 'doubled practices' where we listen to the attempts of others as they make sense of their lives. It also allows us to resist the seductive qualities of 'too easy' constructs such as 'voice' as we trouble experience itself, which is always already constituted within one 'grand narrative' or another (Lather, 2001, p. 218)" (ibid., 903).

8. Ibid., 903.

9. By "population pools" I refer to groupings of students, like a high school, an ethnic group, a neighborhood, etc.

10. "Groupthink occurs when a homogenous highly cohesive group is so concerned with maintaining unanimity that they fail to evaluate all their alternatives and options" (Contexts of Communication, "Groupthink," *http://oregonstate.edu/instruct/theory/grpthink.html*). See also Irving Janis, *Groupthink: Psychological Studies of Policy Decisions and Fiascoes* (Boston: Houghton Mifflin, 1982).

11. According to the State of Washington Department of Personnel, for example, competencies are defined as "the measurable or observable knowledge, skills, abilities, and behaviors (KSABs) critical to successful job performance" (Washington State Department of Personnel, "Competencies," *http://www.dop.wa.gov/strategichr/workforceplanning/ competencies/pages/default.aspx*).

Sticky Faith, Youth Worker Edition

Practical Ideas to Nurture Long-Term Faith in Teenagers

Kara E. Powell, Brad M. Griffin, and Cheryl A. Crawford

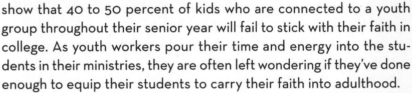

Many of the statistics you read about teenagers and faith can be alarming. Recent studies show that 40 to 50 percent of kids who are connected to a youth group throughout their senior year will fail to stick with their faith in college. As youth workers pour their time and energy into the students in their ministries, they are often left wondering if they've done enough to equip their students to carry their faith into adulthood.

Fuller Youth Institute has done extensive research in the area of youth ministry and teenage development. In *Sticky Faith*, the team at FYI presents youth workers with both a theological/philosophical framework and practical programming ideas to develop long-term faith in teenagers. Each chapter presents a summary of FYI's quantitative and qualitative research, along with the implications of this research, including program ideas suggested and tested by youth ministries nationwide.

This resource will give youth pastors what they need to help foster a faith that sticks with all the teenagers in their group long after they've left the youth room.

Available in stores and online!

Sticky Faith Curriculum for Teenagers

10 Lessons to Nurture Faith beyond High School

Kara E. Powell and Brad M. Griffin

Both national leaders with broad spheres of influence as well as local, grassroots practitioners are waking up to the reality that 50 percent of graduating seniors struggle deeply with their faith in college. Offering a few special "Senior Seminars" or giving seniors a "graduation Bible" and hoping for the best are both too little and too late.

Fuller Youth Institute's research confirms that it's never too early to start developing faith that continues to grow and lasts. *Sticky Faith* gives youth workers both a theological/philosophical framework and a host of practical programming ideas to develop long-term faith in teenagers.